WOMEN MINISTERS

Edited by
Judith L.
Weidman

1817

HARPER & ROW, PUBLISHERS, SAN FRANCISCO
Cambridge, Hagerstown, New York, Philadelphia
London, Mexico City, São Paulo, Singapore, Sydney

WOMEN MINISTERS. Copyright © 1981, 1985 by Harper & Row, Publishers, Inc. All rights reserved. Printed in the United States of America. No part of this book may be used or reproduced in any manner whatsoever without written permission except in the case of brief quotations embodied in critical articles and reviews. For information address Harper & Row, Publishers, Inc., 10 East 53rd Street, New York NY 10022. Published simultaneously in Canada by Fitzhenry & Whiteside, Limited, Toronto.

Designed by Donna Davis

Library of Congress Cataloging in Publication Data
Main entry under title:

Women ministers.
   1. Women clergy—Addresses, essays, lectures.
I. Weidman, Judith L.
BV676.W55   1981   253'.2   84-48232
ISBN 0-06-069293-6

---

85 86 87 88 89 MPC 10 9 8 7 6 5 4 3 2 1

CONTENTS

1

INTRODUCTION

Judith L. Weidman

Myrtle Saylor felt the call to preach at age ten as she listened to the lofty words of the communion ritual. When she got home from church that day, she burst into tears, explaining to her concerned father, "I'm crying because I'm not a little boy."

Somehow she knew.

In all of her fifty-year ministry, which spanned all the deliberations on the ordination of women in the Methodist Church and its predecessor bodies, she was never made a full member of "the club."

Votes by the Methodist Episcopal Church in the early 1920s to license and ordain women as local preachers were over-turned in 1939 at the time of union with the southern church. In 1956, when full clergy rights were granted to women, Myrtle Saylor Speer was told by her bishop that the first woman member of the annual conference must be a seminary

The Rev. Judith L. Weidman is editor/director of Religious News Service in New York City. Prior to assuming her present position, she was the communications officer of the United Methodist Board of Higher Education and Ministry. Her background also includes writing for the public and church press and editing denominational curriculum materials. Ms. Weidman has been active in the Yoke-fellows Prison Ministry and is the editor of Christian Feminism: Visions of a New Humanity. *She is a graduate of DePauw University and Duke Divinity School.*

graduate. It did not help that when she had applied to Garrett Biblical Institute in 1915, she had been told they didn't enroll women. It made no difference that she had then gone to the Chicago Training School, an institution that later merged with Garrett, and that she is considered a graduate of that seminary.

Her fortunes shifted in 1972 with the arrival of a new bishop. She finally was made a full member of the conference. But by then it was just an honor; she had already retired.

This story could not happen now, yet it is hardly ancient history. The last of the mainline Protestant denominations did not approve ordination of women until 1976. That was the Episcopal Church, where the issue wrenched longest and hardest. The American Lutheran Church and the Lutheran Church in America voted to ordain women in 1970. The Southern Baptist Convention and the Presbyterian Church, U.S., took the step in 1964; the Methodist Church and the United Presbyterian Church, U.S.A., voted to ordain in 1956.

The first woman to be ordained was a Congregationist, Antoinette Brown, in 1853; so the successor denomination, the United Church of Christ, can be said to have led the way. The American Baptists and Disciples of Christ both record the ordination of women in the late 1800s.[1] Those early women were the exception, however. The story of women in ministry in mainline Protestantism began in earnest in the 1970s. During that decade enrollment of women in seminaries doubled, from about 10 percent to just over 21 percent on the average. And although the rate of growth slowed in the early 1980s, the trend was still upward, with 24.4 percent by 1983.[2] In certain cases the figures were much more dramatic. Union Theological Seminary in New York City was one of several liberal schools whose enrollment of women climbed to more than 50 percent during the 1970s.

The percentage of ordained women within denominations also made a dramatic leap. For example, from 1971–78 there was a 300 percent increase in the number of ordained women in the United Presbyterian Church. The actual *numbers*, however, provide a caution to the percentages game: Ordained Presbyterian women increased from 103 to only 409 during and found none available at the time.[5]

Currently, a major program effort on behalf of clergy-women is being developed ecumenically through the Women in Ministry Project of the National Council of Churches. The program seeks to develop curriculum that can be used with church members in a variety of settings in a two-day program. Its aim is gigantic: preparing churches for women pastors, which means fundamental attitude change.

Research behind the program reveals that attitudes are changed through the senses, not through logic; and that stereotypes cluster. So attitudes affecting women are often coupled with general resistance to change. Many times, to be human is to protect oneself from new experiences. The curriculum, then, helps participants explore the ways in which new experiences can enrich their lives, not detract. Storytelling is used. "The Silver Stream," an audio-visual presentation developed for the program, makes use of allegory to talk about change.

Systemic change, which is at the heart of the matter, is slow in coming. The question of salaries is a case in point. Figures released by the Board of Pensions of the United Church of Christ show that in 1978 the salaries of its male clergy rose an average of 7 percent, whereas the salaries of its female clergy rose an average of only 4.8 percent.[6] It may be possible to find some comfort in the suggestion that those figures undoubtedly reflect, in part, the youth of many of the women and thus their placement in smaller, less affluent settings. But women often fare no better, even in more comparable situations. In the California-Nevada Conference of the United Methodist Church, for example, a statistical report based on 1978 data reveals that salaries of clergywomen entering the conference since 1970 averaged 16 percent lower than salaries of white clergymen entering at the same time.[7]

A study of eleven Protestant denominations released by the National Council of Churches in 1984 shows the situation is not improving for women in the 1980s. The average salary for all clergy is $20,790. Salaries for women, however, averaged only $14,000 to $16,000.[8]

The ravages of sexism obviously have visited ordained

women with real force. The figures are clear, but a more
elusive issue is impact. How are women faring in the church
and what difference is their ministry making?

In a modest survey by a doctoral student of twenty-eight
churches, half of which were served by women and half of
which were served by men, responses indicated that the laity
saw their pastors in quite similar terms. But when these pastors (men and women) were compared to the previous pastors of those same churches (all men), there was a difference.
The churches with women pastors tended to see their former
pastors much differently than churches that had been served
by men in both instances. Areas cited included a more personal preaching style, greater approachability, and a stronger
tendency to include lay people in decision-making.[9] In other
words, the laity's perception of the shape and style of ministry does change after being served by a woman.

In general, the *experience* of having a woman pastor seems
to prove less traumatic than the *idea*.[10] An American Baptist
study offers this analysis:

> As concerns acceptance within the church, all differ-
> ences between men and women tend to diminish. The
> level of acceptance reported by the women tends to
> change considerably more than that reported by men. It
> is possible that this pattern indicates that women minis-
> ters themselves settle down and feel more secure. How-
> ever, there is also evidence to suggest that the churches
> also change somewhat from the time the woman min-
> ister first arrives to a point in time where they have
> become accustomed to her. In a few instances, the
> churches at first felt somewhat stigmatized in having to
> call a woman as pastor. However, after discovering that
> the organization did not fall apart after the woman
> arrived on the scene, the presence of the woman in their
> pulpit became a badge of honor and a symbol that they
> were in the forefront of a social movement within the
> churches in American society.[11]

The question of acceptance first arises for the clergywoman
during the long process of being approved for ordination. It

continues as she seeks placement in a church and follows her even as she assumes the responsibilities of a pastor of a congregation. A United Methodist study published in 1980 indicates that for many women the first steps into ordained ministry, when they first encountered "the system," were far from satisfying. The same was true of their seminary days. Once on the job, however, they reported a higher level of satisfaction. As for "overt discrimination," 20 percent reported a great deal of difficulty, while 63.5 percent reported low levels of difficulty.[12]

The great strength of women clergy is their own sense of a call from God. This factor as a prime source of motivation showed up in a single denominational study and was subsequently confirmed by an inquiry which cut across denominational lines.[13]

Letty Russell, an astute observer of this scene, insists that the issue of acceptance of clergywomen is a theological matter. "The question," she says, "is not just a matter of adding up the contributions women make to the ministry of the church and deducing the inconveniences they present for a particular committee on ordination or ministerial relations. . . . Ultimately it is a matter of how we do our theology, of how we choose our questions, and how we arrive at answers as we think about God's call to mission and ministry in church and society."[14]

From this perspective, women are no longer a problem to be studied. Rather, they are participants in the task of defining ministry and defining the church's future.

The issue for Roman Catholic women, of course, foments in an entirely different milieu. The early 1970s were times of awakening consciousness for women religious in the American Catholic church, too; but a decade later the results have been the opposite of their Protestant counterparts.

In 1972 the Leadership Conference of Women Religious, the powerful coordinating body representing 90 percent of the nuns in the United States, declared its solidarity with women's liberation. Within two years it was on record further as supporting the principle that all the ministries of the church should be open to women.[15] Study books were issued, a women's ordination conference was held, and various subgroups sprang up.

But momentum was interrupted in 1976 by a papal declaration that the exclusion of women from the priesthood is founded on Christ's own practice in choosing the apostles and subsequent church tradition, and therefore cannot be changed. As one theologian explains, "To introduce a Christian priesthood of women accepts, at least by implication, the idea that the founder of Christianity, Christ himself, could be wrong on a central point of his teaching practice."[16] Those who come out on the other side take much the same tact as Protestants of priestly tradition did before them: that the central issue with Christ is not his maleness, but his humanity.

The 1980s have not eased the Vatican's position. In 1983 a decree was issued regarding nuns, which has been summarized as telling them "they must get back into their habits, back into convents, back into the schools and hospitals."[17]

While the issue of women in the Roman Catholic Church is not amenable to democratic processes, it is interesting to note that a 1982 Gallup Poll showed that 44 percent of American Catholics favored ordination of women. While a minority opinion, the figure had risen from 29 percent in 1974.[18]

Rosemary Ruether, a leading Catholic theologian, says of the issue, "It is likely that a long seedtime must set in."[19] Meanwhile, she asks with Eleanor McLaughlin: "Is it enough simply to be incorporated into paradigms of ordained ministry shaped by males for many hundreds of years in hierarchical molds intended to exclude women? Or must women, by their very presence, reshape the ministry into forms that are more open, pluralistic and dialogic?"[20]

In the chapters that follow, the authors attempt to do pastoral theology, addressing precisely these questions. In the two opening chapters, the varied personal and professional experiences of women in minstry are highlighted: a young woman recently out of seminary confronts the issue of "being in charge" as the sole pastor of a suburban congregation of 400 members; a second-career woman discusses the gifts women bring to the special needs of a small rural church.

Good preaching is not just a concern of women, to be sure.

But the author of one of the chapters on preaching suggests that the recovery of the biblical art of storytelling holds particular promise for the woman pastor. Another writer, a woman who practiced her gift of speaking in the classroom until the fullness of time, shares her hopes for women who come out of the strong preaching tradition of the black church. In a related chapter on worship, an Episcopal woman finds it altogether fitting that women should serve as priests at the Table of our Lord, and recounts some of her denomination's struggle with the issue.

A ministry of presence—that's how another author describes her counseling assignment in a downtown church, where the needs of people daily threatened to overwhelm her. But she found strength for her role because, as a woman, she was raised to be sensitive to relationships. The chapter on evangelism was "birthed" in the secular context of Southern California. The author's unique use of the imagery of childbearing illustrates her hope of new life for the church.

In an essay on the educational task of the church, one writer rehearses the tradition of Christian education as "women's work." Ordained women, she asserts, have an opportunity to do education in the broader context of the church's total program. Social ministry is seen through the eyes of a woman who serves part-time in a parish and part-time in a social service agency. She points to the rift in relations between men and women (indeed, between the maleness and femaleness in all of us) as the source of many social ills. In another chapter, the task of enabling lay people in the congregation is treated from the perspective of a Hispanic woman in Puerto Rico operating in a *machista* culture.

"Spiritual formation" is a phrase that has become shorthand for a renewed emphasis on spiritual life in the church. One author talks about her own renewal journey and the difference this made in the life of her congregation. Another author talks about her own experience of healing and the ministry that has emerged for her in this area. A nun reflects on her ministry to women in prison. She mourns the limitations imposed on that ministry by the Catholic Church's refusal to ordain women to the priesthood.

In the closing chapter, a clergy couple offer a personal and professional model for this new form of ministry that links two clergypersons in marriage and ministry.

What these women, and one man, have to say is certainly not the last word. But it comes as an *authentic* word, written at the beginning of this decade from their pastorates amid tornadoes, sick children, arriving refugees, and a heavy overlay of public demand, while nearly making such a book impossible at the same time made it necessary.

Notes

1. Constant H. Jacquet, Jr., Ed., *Yearbook, of American and Candian Churches 1979* (Nashville: Abingdon Press, 1979), p. 266.

2. Jacquet, *Yearbook 1984*, p. 271. Detailed information on seminary enrollment can be found in the *ATS Fact Book*, published yearly by the Association of Theological Schools, Vandalia, Ohio.

3. These figures on numbers of clergywomen and other figures used throughout this chapter were supplied by denominational headquarters in telephone calls and/or internal documents.

4. Jackson W. Carroll, Barbara Hargrove, Adair T. Lummis, eds., *Women of the Cloth* (San Francisco: Harper & Row, 1983), p. 107.

5. *The Women's Pulpit*, journal of the International Association of Women Ministers, Jan.–Mar. 1980, pp. 1, 8.

6. *Keeping You Posted*, newsletter published by the United Church of Christ, Oct. 1, 1979, p. 1.

7. *Journal and Yearbook*, California-Nevada Conference, United Methodist Church, 1979, p. 166.

8. Jacquet, *Yearbook 1984*, p. 267.

9. Susan Murch Morrison, "Ministry Shaped by Hope . . . Toward Wholeness: The Woman as Ordained Minister," D. Min. thesis, Wesley Theological Seminary, Washington, D.C., May 1979, p. 106.

10. See also Edward C. Lehman, Jr., "The Minister-At-Large Program: An Evaluation," report issued by the Vocation Agency, the United Presbyerian Church in the U.S.A., May 1981.

11. Edward C. Lehman, Jr., *Project Swim: A Study of Women in Ministry* (Valley

Forge, Penn.: The Ministers Council, American Baptist Church, 1979), p. 19. See also, Carroll, Hargrove, and Lummis, *Women of the Cloth*, pp. 152–59.

12. Harry Hale, Jr., Morton King, and Doris Moreland Jones, *New Witnesses: United Methodist Clergywomen* (Nashville: United Methodist Board of Higher Education and Ministry, 1980), pp. 57–59.

13. *Ibid.*, p. 51. See also Carroll, Hargrove, and Lummis, *Women of the Cloth*, p. 107.

14. Judith L. Weidman, ed., *Christian Feminism: Visions of a New Humanity* (San Francisco: Harper & Row, 1984), p. 75.

15. Rosemary Ruether and Eleanor McLaughlin, eds., *Women of Spirit* (New York: Simon and Schuster, 1979), p. 375.

16. Mary O'Connell, "Why Don't Catholics Have Priests?" *U.S. Catholic* (Jan. 1984), p. 8.

17. Kathleen Whalen Fitzgerald, "The Papal Power Game," *The Christian Century* (May 30, 1984), p. 574.

18. O'Connell, "Why Don't Catholics Have Priests?" p. 12.

19. Ruether and McLaughlin, *Women of Spirit*, p. 381.

20. *Ibid.*, p. 28.

GROWING TOWARD EFFECTIVE MINISTRY

M. Helene Pollock

1962. I was a teenage girl in Fremont, Nebraska. With family conflicts and adolescent growing pains in my heart, I wept to myself in church, "Dear Lord, please understand." It may have been the beginning of my call to ministry, but at that time I had no words for my feelings.

1967. A coed majoring in Spanish, I set off for Bogota, Colombia, eager for the experience of a different culture. There I found a new self and a new inner compulsion for justice.

1969. I began my studies at Union Theological Seminary in

The Rev. M. Helene Pollock is pastor of First Presbyterian Church in Darby, Pennsylvania. Prior to her present pastorate she served in New York City as a youth worker in the South Bronx, as assistant pastor in a Spanish-speaking church in East Harlem, and as assistant pastor in a Brooklyn parish. She is a graduate of Beloit College and Union Theological Seminary in New York.

New York City, looking for time and space to explore issues of faith and social justice.

1972. I became a "reverend" and began full-time church employment as an assistant pastor in New York.

1976. I became the sole pastor of a 400-member Presbyterian church in a blue-collar suburb of Philadelphia. I was "in charge" and expected to function competently and effectively.

This is my story, but the realities belong to many of us. We are young women, growing up in our home churches, members of mainline denominations. We struggle through many personal questions, in a wide variety of settings. And then the time comes when we are on our own. We are out of school; we are employed. Some of us are fortunate: We are able to grow and develop through challenging, full-time, paid ministry. Others work in less satisfying or temporary situations. All of us are committed to do our best while breaking into a job market that receives us reluctantly, if at all. But whatever our situation, we are now on our own —in charge of our own career, our own area of job responsibility.

Leaving school, beginning a career, becoming established as a professional person—it's an exciting time of life. It's like leaving Egypt and starting out on the road toward the Promised Land. But the desert is vast and dry. Our road stretches out, weaving its way into a distant wilderness, with few landmarks and no road map. This is a time of countless questions, all unanswered. We need information and practical suggestions; we need definitions and guidelines. We need to discover what is expected of us, what skills are required, and whether we have these skills. We are trying hard; we need to feel that we are accomplishing something. We need to feel that we are effective.

"Am I effective?" The question has been with us before. In previous employment situations we tried to be effective. As students, completing a test or a paper, we received a grade—an estimate of our effectiveness in that particular subject area. Now in the first years of professional ministry, as we try ourselves out in new situations, as we test the limits of our capabilities, we are developing a new sense of effectiveness. We are seeking to be competent in our own field, in our own way. As we test ourselves out, a natural tendency is to compare ourselves with other ministers. The differences seem obvious. While we are full of enthusiasm and new possibilities, they appear to be in a rut. They carry on doggedly day after day, year after year; they seem so uninspired. Under their leadership the church seems incredibly tradition bound, narrow-minded, stymied. We wonder why the leaders of the church aren't able to *do* more, *change* more, make the church more like the dynamic fellowship of the New Testament. So we fantasize. We dream about how *we* could change things, how things could be different "if only they weren't in charge." As we do this, we find that our perspective on the church has changed. New ideas are taking shape for us. We are beginning to develop a sense of "effectiveness," what it might mean, what it should mean.

However, so much is going on within us during these first few years that we aren't free to devote our full energy to developing our effectiveness. Our outer world has changed greatly (from seminary to church work); our inner world is changing, too. So we struggle with new internal conflicts as we face a new form of the old question, "Who am I?"

"I'm the pastor, but who am I?" The question is very difficult. Lacking experience and self-confidence, we struggle hard to come to terms with our new professional selves. This struggle is particularly acute for the sole pastor. When you're in charge, you're "it." No other pastor can buffer the demands and reactions of the people; no other pastor can be blamed for the problems. You're it—but what does it really mean to be "it"?

The people of the church send out many signals, in their own way telling the pastor what it means to be "it." However, their messages are not always helpful, even though they mean well. For example, church people treat the new woman minister in a very special way. She seems unique; they want to set her apart. During the process of job interviews and upon her arrival in the new parish, she is continually singled out and held up as an example of extraordinariness. She is listened to in a special way. She is sought out by all kinds of people; she may even be interviewed by reporters and invited to talk shows.

In the course of all this specialness the new pastor is tempted to expect too much of herself. Inside she is scared. She feels she must prove herself. But it is not enough to prove that "I can do it"; she must demonstrate once and for all that "we women can do it!" She has become ambassador to the world on behalf of all women and all women ministers. In this grandiose task a woman is tempted to overemphasize the differences between herself and other human beings. She may labor under the illusion that by being female she is immune to the weaknesses and temptations which plague male ministers. Her "set-apartness" from other women may also lead to a sense of isolation and an ambivalence toward traditional female roles.

At the same time that the people say, "You're special, you're unique," the female minister elicits powerful archetypal images in the minds of the congregation. As they open themselves up to God in the context of worship, they imbue the pastor with almost mystical overtones. What touches them is a fleeting image, a new experience—"the great earth mother," "the sweet dutiful daughter," or some other female image has been born in them. As they allow themselves to be vulnerable before God, they open the potential for new religious experiences. They also expose themselves as deeply vulnerable before the pastor, which tends to put more distance between pastor and people. It is difficult for the new pastor to figure out what is going on, what the people want, and who she is in the midst of it all.

My first awareness of the "nurturing mother" archetype came one day when I visited a church member's home, and he expressed surprise at my slender build. Before the visit he had never seen me without my pulpit robe. Somehow he had assumed that I was heavyset. Later, when I sorted things through, I realized that he had been caught up in the "nurturing mother" archetype during worship, and consequently he expected me to look like a hefty earth mother. Over time I have become accustomed to such experiences, but initially they were confusing and disorienting.

The heavy load of pastoral care can also become a source of insecurity. I had been in my office no more than an hour on my first day of work when I received word of a serious automobile accident that had put a church member in intensive care. During the next few weeks I faced countless new pastoral situations, each of which carried its own share of human suffering. However caring a person may have been before becoming a pastor, chances are she or he has never before faced so many people in need. It is only natural that we experience doubts: "Can I really do this job?"

Many other factors intensify the insecurity of the new pastor. Job contracts are unclear in the church, especially with sole pastors For example, church members have come to assume that the pastor will serve as the church's figurehead. They expect a certain demeanor and style of dress; they look forward to various ceremonial appearances of the pastor. But they usually cannot articulate these expectations. The new pastor realizes that the people are expecting many things, but it is hard to know exactly what. If these unarticulated expectations are violated, the people are quick to comment or criticize, though they will seldom voice their feelings directly to the pastor.

It's a lot all at once, becoming the pastor. The pastor is the one people turn to in the crisis situations of life. The pastor is expected to "act like a pastor," but nobody spells out how a pastor is supposed to act, or exactly what a pastor is supposed to do. And the pastor carries the burden of this insecurity alone. Nobody can magically unravel the confusing new situation; nobody can eliminate the new pastor's lack of experience in one fell swoop.

Sooner or later all female ministers find loneliness an inevitable part of their experience. Because we are leaders, we have stepped away from the crowd. We are special, but we are also alone, in a new way. We stand apart. At times we find ourselves totally cut off from that comfortable former self who was "just one of the girls." Our experience is like that of the new elder chairing a committee who becomes embroiled in controversy for the first time: Suddenly that elder cannot fade into the back pew any more. Leadership brings visibility and vulnerability.

Clearly, the first few years of ministry are a time of trial. We cope as best we can, even though our coping style may not be completely adequate for the situation. Sometimes we revert to old, outgrown behavior patterns—our "back-up style." As women shaped by this culture, our tendency very often is to regress into dependency or to fall back into an earlier, so-called feminine state of childlike dependency. During the early years of ministry our insecurity may very well tempt us toward such immature behavior patterns as living through others, mirroring others without developing our own sense of self, and putting ourselves down. When our effectiveness has been called into question in new ways, we come to feel insecure and unworthy.

Even as we hide our vulnerability from the people of the church (after all, they look to *us* for strength), we find ourselves deeply vulnerable in our lives outside the church. We seek stable, reassuring relationships which will affirm us and help us discover our own sense of effectiveness and self-worth. This is a time of real stress for ministers' marriages. Single pastors have their own difficulty in finding deep, affirming relationships. Whether married or single, the pastor seeks a mentor—an older, more experienced person who can provide guidance. But such people are hard to find. The more vulnerable we feel, the more reluctant we are to be open, the more afraid of our own dependency needs.

This painful struggle is heightened by the cleavage in our culture between the women's liberation movement and the traditionalist view of women's roles. Like the culture as a whole, our churches are caught in this cleavage. The woman pastor faces these issues head-on, day in and day out. In spite of the insecurity she may be experiencing, she is frequently called upon to speak out against biblical and theological interpretations which reinforce a destructive passivity and dependency in women. For example, I have often been involved in discussions of the creation accounts in

Genesis in which I had to counteract these assumptions: (1)
Since woman was taken from man's rib, she must derive her
worth from a man; she cannot have worth on her own; and
(2) since Eve was created after Adam, woman is of less worth
than man. Myths like these permeate our church life, and
they need to be challenged.

In the course of this struggle, as we experience the pain,
the challenge, and the insecurity of our early years in ministry, there comes a point when our old patterns wither. They
are ready to be shed, like a snake's skin. In my case the "old
me" that needed to die was a hungry, devouring "bad mother." She could not help me to be an effective pastor. The day
came when she was ready to be shed. That day I wrote the
following notes in my journal:

The Bad Mother Who Must Die

She is superior to everyone.

She is omniscient (all knowing)—especially when it
comes to the feelings and deepest reality of others.

She lives through others.

She has no feelings of her own, but merely "shadows"
others.

She sees everyone as an extension of herself.

She does not know how to love—only how to control
(or be controlled).

She is terribly hurt inside, because others have not
come through for her impossible expectations.

She desperately needs to be needed. She relates to
others who she fantasizes as "dependent."

She fears not being needed, and thereby rejected.

She can receive something from girls and boys,
but not from men and women.

Through the dying of the old and the birthing of the new
our professional identity is born. Gradually we find a means
here and there of grasping what is happening; we develop
definitions, we find sources of strength. True, we are set
apart, we are leaders, we stand alone. At the same time, we
are still human beings. We recognize both our potential and

our limitations. We are exhilarated by the possibilities of the pastorate, but we are disheartened by the many realities that cannot be changed. We are mortal, yet we are in touch with the eternal.

When it comes to the discovery of humanness, church members can be wonderfully helpful to the pastor. The professional issues facing lay people may take a different form from those of the pastor, but the underlying human issues are the same for all of us. In many cases it is the old people, the handicapped, and the sick whose insights are most helpful. Many of them have discovered God's unique perspective on limits, which contrasts sharply with the values of the world. They live with insecurity—the insecurity of their limitations and the insecurity of approaching death. They can teach the new pastor about life. They can also open the pastor's eyes to God's word:

> But we have this treasure in earthen vessels, to
> show that the transcendent power belongs to God and
> not to us. We are afflicted in every way, but not
> crushed; perplexed, but not driven to despair;
> persecuted, but not forsaken; struck down, but not
> destroyed; always carrying in the body the death of
> Jesus, so that the life of Jesus may be manifested in
> our bodies.   [2 Cor. 4:7–11]

When through the grace of God a pastor comes to grips with her or his own humanness, yet knows how to use the special "pastor role," that person has laid the groundwork for a real discovery of personal effectiveness in the ministry.

I began the current phase of my professional journey four years ago, when I was installed as *the* pastor of First Presbyterian Church in Darby, Pennsylvania. I soon discovered that the church needed an institutional mechanic. Like other institutions, it couldn't just run by itself. As the pastor, I was the mechanic: I was in charge of preventive maintenance as well as emergency repairs; I had the job of greasing all the parts.

It took a long time for me to learn the "church machine"

as a whole—that is, to consider all aspects of the church's program and to be aware of the number of wheels that really needed greasing. Here are a few:

Worship services, including those reaching the regular congregation, those for shut-ins, and those aimed at friends and neighbors of the church.

All aspects of the caring program of the church, such as prayer support, emergency food, and counseling.

Educational, social, and outreach activities of the parish.

Financial management.

The church staff: secretary, custodian, organist, choir director, paid soloists, and a student assistant.

The physical plant (two old but well-maintained buildings)—its use, its upkeep, its potential.

Relations with the community—mine as a professional individual and the church's presence in the struggles of the neighborhood, as well as alliances with other churches and civic groups.

While taking stock of all of this, I also found myself considering the church's history, something that was especially important in a stable congregation of many older people. I needed to understand the style of worship and programming that the people had grown accustomed to through the years. I needed to become aware of some of the personalities (lay and clergy) who had shaped the church's program, and those who continued to have a high stake in certain aspects of it. I searched out the resources of church and community—people, property, financial—assessing both their present condition and future potential. Another challenge was to unravel the family relationships, clans, and cliques which were affecting people's patterns of church participation. Finally, I needed to relate to the church staff and develop a clear breakdown of job responsibilities. What would be my relationships to all these various people?

During this initial period of listening, learning, and developing relationships, my sensitivities were often wounded and my mind boggled. Why did people do things the way they did? Why did they assume what they were assuming? Our working-class neighborhood was divided into "zones," with different racial groups, teenage gangs, churches, and social classes carving out their own territories. This was hard for me to understand and accept. Within the church I was puzzled by the relationships between people of different generations. I couldn't tell who really held the purse strings. Where were the people who really cared about the needy? Who in the congregation was eager to grow in personal faith? Did the congregation want to grow in numbers? What would meet the needs of those members who had become inactive?

Along with all the other unanswered questions came the mystery of finances. How much money did it take to keep things running? Was the budget realistic? Could we meet our obligations? These questions began to confront me with increasing persistance. It soon became obvious that the church's record-keeping system needed revamping so we would have a better idea where we stood. Neither the church treasurer nor I had studied bookkeeping, but with a little common sense we were able to get the books in order. Eventually we were able to resurrect the dormant finance committee and devise a quarterly reporting system for the session.

About this time several church members began asking what we should do about the organ. It was not a new problem; the church had vacillated between repair and replacement for twenty years before my arrival. At one point several years before, the decision had been made to buy a new organ. A down payment was made and then lost when the decision was reversed. So it was a ticklish situation.

My initial approach was to draw together a representative committee to study the options. We did our work over the course of several months, and in the process I learned a lot about organs. It took several meetings of the session to digest the material, but the final decision was to rebuild our present pipe organ at a cost of $23,000. That figure scared me; I didn't know the first thing about raising money.

At the same time I was working with the organ committee, I went looking for every available resource on fund raising. A friendly presbytery executive helped fill me in on
some of the basics, and I consulted members of the parish
with experience in finances. We formed an executive committee of the financial campaign, and, as we began to meet,
they remembered past fund-raising efforts of the church
which had been successful. These memories were important
as we began the effort of developing and "selling" a new
campaign.

The presbytery executive suggested we engage a professional fund raiser to help us with our drive. I was all in favor
of the idea, but it was soundly defeated at a congregational
meeting. It was frightening but true: Our little committee
would be heading a major fund-raising drive on our own.
We drew in some people from other churches who had used
professionals in this field and took careful note of their experiences.

As our plans finally emerged, we set our goal at not
$23,000 but $40,000, which would include money for our denomination's mission fund drive and needed maintenance
work on our buildings as well as the organ. It was a package
that spoke to a variety of needs and eliminated a sense of
competition among the organ enthusiasts, the missionary-
minded folks, and those with a rightful concern for our
physical plant.

We mounted a "name the campaign" drive in the church,
complete with prizes, and combined the winning entries
into a "Come Together" theme for the 3M's (music, maintenance, and mission). We developed a 3M logo, held a kickoff
banquet, recruited teams for an every-member visitation,
trained our callers—and we exceeded our goal!

I can still remember driving home that evening after the
campaign pledges had been counted. I felt the growth and
challenge within my own heart even more than I felt it in
the church. Like many women, I had been reticent, insecure,
and intimidated all my life when dealing with finances. Nobody in the church knew how frightened and lonely I had
felt while trying to wade through our financial morass.

In time the church finances settled into predictable, routine patterns. I was even approached by a new seminary graduate who felt she needed a female role model in the area of financial management. "Me of all people," I thought. But I felt she could benefit from involvement with our finance committee, and they were agreeable. This brief experience helped her grow in self-confidence to the point where she was able to go through job interviews without panicking when financial matters were discussed.

After four years of experience in this church I no longer find the various administrative questions as all-encompassing as they were at first. Most of the tasks have become routine. But sometimes I get tired; it is too much of a load. Then I feel the need to stand back and evaluate.

I am responsible for evaluating my work *by* myself, *with* myself. I am ultimately responsible *to* my self, in light of my accountability to God. That means that I must take time away from work to get the support I need, and I must find the time alone so that I can know where I stand. It is crucial to develop personal discipline in the parish ministry. It is necessary to say no to the church and the church people for a period of time each day, each week, and each year, in order to be refreshed and renewed. While the minister relaxes and prays, energy is rechanneled so that it can be reborn another day.

Sometimes it is hard to admit that overwork is a sin, but it is. Overwork is destructive of the temple of the Holy Spirit. It dims the vision, sharpens the temper, kills creativity, and deadens spiritual sensitivity. Some of us in parish ministry are tempted to try to do everything. Long after forty hours of work have been accomplished, we're still at the church "just trying to finish things up." But the simple truth is that "things" in the parish are never finished.

It is impossible to know who I am and what God has called me to do without deep, supportive relationships. Time away from the church needs to be spent developing these relationships. The need to make choices about our time often curtails painful conflicts between church and family or friends. Yet the relationships are worth all the struggle. I could never minister without the support of my closest friends and family. In my experience the times of greatest personal stress have been right after relocation, before new relationships have had time to develop and when old relationships are fading. At such times I have sought out extra support from professional Christian counselors. I am always in need of support and sharing with other clergywomen and professional women. Presently I also participate in a coed clergy support group that meets biweekly. These relationships help me remember who I am on a daily basis.

On a broader level self-evaluation involves asking, "What am I doing?" and "What is the church doing?" It is necessary to stand back and develop a new vision of what it means to be the church of Jesus Christ. From time to time I am challenged to a new vision through sharing with Christians whose lives are different from mine but who share a common ministry in this global village. I recently returned to Colombia, where I had lived as a student, to visit one of my Colombian sisters who is now a Roman Catholic nun. After living and sharing with her and the other sisters, I discovered a new perspective on the church's ministry, a new sense of urgency in helping the needy, and a new vision of hope for the world.

Another time my vision was renewed when our church was visitied by a Presbyterian church leader from South Korea. She stayed with our congregation and worked side by side with me for a month in a program administered by our denomination. At the time I felt overloaded with the activities of our church's 125th anniversary. Yet through the relationship with my Korean visitor I discovered a new perspective on Christian ministry. She shared a deep spirituality and prayer life that were intimately tied to an unbending commitment to the human rights struggle. As I began to see our local issues in a worldwide context, my problems as pastor became less overwhelming. I asked myself again, "What am I doing?" and "What is the church doing?" I discovered that my answers were changing as my perspective broadened.

As my vision broadens, I turn to evaluate my stewardship

of time. Usually I find that I have spent too much time greasing the wheels and not enough time reaching out to the
Lord. As I struggle with this tendency, I try to find ways to
affirm the healthy, reasonable, noncompulsive accomplish-
ments of each day. Then I find I'm not so tempted to keep on
accomplishing. I have developed a time chart for recording
my work hours, using the "Toward Improvement of Ministry" materials developed by the vocation agency of my denomination. The various pastoral functions are broken down
into thirty-four categories on a pad of ledger paper. Each
evening before I go home I recount my work for that day,
breaking it into such categories as worship preparation, office work, church school support, home visits, attention to
various committees, counseling, presbytery responsibilities,
planning and evaluation, personal study, sermon preparation, and so on. I pretend that the paper is an accepting, ap-
proving supervisor as I enjoy the satisfaction of "reporting
in" my hours. I use this system to give myself permission to
cut back when I have been working excessively. This record
also provides cumulative data for evaluating my time priori-
ties.

Whenever I stand back and look at my work in a broader
perspective, I locate certain areas that deserve particular attention. Some time ago I could see that the worship service
lacked vitality. I felt a need to improve my worship leadership and preaching, but I didn't know what specific areas to
work on. It was hard to ask the people of the church since
they have been taught to sit passively through the worship
service without reacting to anything. I also found them reluctant to voice negative feelings directly to me as pastor.
Yet how could I improve without some feedback from
them?

I decided to invite several church members who did not
have pressing family commitments to talk with me after the
service about our shared worship experience. The discussions have been a big help. We continue to meet each Sunday with brown bag lunches for an hour and a half after the
service. We talk about what happened during that hour; we
also try to find a relationship between the Scripture and our
daily lives. The group has helped me understand the nature

of the spirituality of the people, and it has helped the people put their feelings about the worship service into words. It has also helped me find concrete ways to improve the Sunday morning worship service.

Another time when I stood back to evaluate, I was struck by the static nature of the interpersonal relationships in the church. For the most part, these patterns are so set that they never change. The pastor must work with the patterns, not against them, yet I felt the need to do something to bring more life to them. It began to seem important for me to provide a model of openness so that people could be more open, too. After all, Jesus was open to everybody—from leper to Pharisee—with a healing message of God's love.

So I decided to step back to evaluate my relationships within the church. I asked myself:

Am I uncomfortable with people I don't know well? If so, am I partial to the "workers" of the church, those who are most frequently in contact with me?

Am I anxious to gain approval? If so, am I partial to the "insiders" who run the church?

Am I still wounded from past experiences when I have been excluded or held back unfairly? If so, am I unduly partial to the "outsiders" of the church and community?

Am I overly concerned about the finances of the parish? If so, am I partial to the large contributors?

Am I seeking to be "built up" by my role as pastor? If so, am I partial to those who show me the greatest deference?

What are my attitudes toward social class? Do I feel uncomfortable with people who have more money or education than myself? Do I tend to feel patronizing toward those of a lower class? Do I feel comfortable with people of all racial and ethnic backgrounds, without stereotyping them in an overly negative or overly positive manner?

Do I tend to experience personality conflicts with certain types of people? If so, am I fair to those persons in my ministry?

Struggling with these questions has led me to shift some of my relationships. I also have organized prayer groups and committees so that people can support each other, rather than always turning to the pastor. And the result has been a new vitality in our congregational life. But it is not enough for me as the pastor to stand back, evaluate myself, develop a new vision, and then start again. A collective vision—and collective evaluation—need to be developed. The lay leaders also need to carry out the process of evaluation, decision making, and planning for the church's future.

Just as a person can be lacking in self-confidence, an entire church can be insecure. Such a collective attitude develops from negative experiences in the past. Perhaps people were asked to take on responsibilities they were not ready to assume, or they may not have been given enough resources and encouragement to complete the task. So they begin to spread the word, "Don't volunteer for anything around here." Perhaps people feel used; they do a lot of work but get little recognition. An undercurrent of silent frustration pervades their participation and inhibits others. Another negative attitude which can develop is the fear of being put down or laughed at. It's hard to express yourself in a group and risk standing alone. And finally, people may feel it's futile to accept leadership in the church since the pastor runs the show anyway. Perhaps the people do not fully understand the polity of the denomination. They may be unclear about which responsibilities are delegated to the session or the governing board and which are reserved for the pastor.

In my experience insecurity is best overcome by accurate information, a climate of acceptance, and positive experiences. I saw early on that the session needed a positive experience in decision making. We also needed to form committees and gain confidence in the committee system. A very practical opportunity soon presented itself. A memorial gift had been received by the church, and the session needed to decide how to spend the money. After a period of discussion and some research our committee recommended purchasing chairs for a particular room. The session seemed relieved at the practicality and concreteness of the recommendation before them and voted unanimously to purchase the chairs. The session had made a decision, people could see the results, and they felt ownership in the process. It gave them something positive to talk about. It gave them experience in the committee system and proof that it works.

I work to help people who accept leadership positions in the church have a positive, growth-producing experience. I spend time with people and get to know them, to learn about their interests, talents, and time commitments. I believe that everyone has a gift to offer, everyone has more gifts to discover—and there is more than enough work to go around. I try to stay in close communication with chairpersons of committees, and I try to provide helpful resources and information. By facilitating communication between the diverse subgroups in the church, I can help avoid overlapping of committees and conflicting programs. As a general rule, my involvement is in the *process* rather than the *outcome* of a committee's work. When it seems advisable, I express my opinion, but not in a coercive way. It is important for me to make people aware of the consequences of actions they may take if they are not already aware of them. But if I truly trust their ability to make a decision, I need to leave the outcome to them.

From time to time the session is faced with a controversial issue. Ideally we should be able to hear ideas as ideas, not as extensions of personalities. We should be able to express an idea, then consider other ideas, and remain open-minded while formulating our final opinion. We should be able to disagree without fearing rejection. We should be able to get angry at each other while remaining in relationship to each other. We should be able to "lose" without losing face. We should be strong enough to express feelings and share from our own lives during the same meeting in which we are vehemently opposed to another person's idea. We should be free enough to ask for additional time to think things over, especially when major decisions are involved. We should gradually develop a shared vision of the church we are called to be, which is built on the insights of individuals. Such a shared vision would make it possible to give up unnecessary traditions and change with the times.

Needless to say, it doesn't always happen this way. When we face controversy together, feelings are often hurt, old wounds are opened, and our raw edges are revealed. One hint of a difficult situation is when an apparently simple, straightforward issue begins to take on irrational overtones. People get heated; voices are raised. Sometimes I am aware of the issues at stake, but other times I have no idea. There are also times when I discover some deep feelings I was not previously aware of. I am often surprised when I find myself getting so emotional.

There is no simple way of dealing with such situations. One way of deflecting some of the irrational feelings is to be sure that there is some informal time at the beginning of the meeting for people to share immediate concerns (if they wish) and blow off some steam. People often arrive at the session with certain frustrations, and they need to relax a lit-tle before being confronted with business. Yet, ironically, as I try to promote informal community building, I run the risk of incurring their hostility by seeming to delay business.

Building a climate of trust where everyone feels a part of the process is a continual challenge. I've found it is impor-tant to express appreciation for each person's ideas, to devel-op noncompetitive procedures, to break large problems into manageable tasks, to cultivate a sense of humor, and to come to session rested and in a positive frame of mind.

As we face the strictures of an inflationary economy, we will be forced to be clearer about our objectives and priori-ties. We will need to evaluate our effectiveness and use our resources more carefully. As a session, we must struggle with the same questions which make up my self-evaluation: "Who are we as a church?" "What are we doing?" "Where are we going?"

At First Presbyterian Church we have found it difficult to concentrate on those broader questions, partly because of our tendency to expend ourselves totally in "business as usual." It takes courage to stand apart from all the business, clear our heads, pray, and seek a new sense of direction. It takes trust between people to admit our total dependence on

God for the answers. But I still believe that somewhere along the way, through the grace of God, congregation and pastor together will discover the hidden treasure within our utterly common, earthen, institutional vessels. And we pray we will be led to take bold new steps, even in our brokenness, our pain, and our pervasive incompleteness. Just as we carry the death of Jesus, we carry the life of Jesus. I hope that life will shine forth as we strive to step back, evaluate, and try once again to "be the church" in these times.

SMALL
CHURCH—
BIG
FAMILY

Virginia Barksdale

A dozen proper Presbyterians were chatting on the front steps when we first found Maxwell Church.[1] My husband John was to preach this time, but all of us knew we were looking at each other for a different reason: They were considering calling *me* to be their minister. We joined the crowd and smiled in the sunshine; some time near eleven o'clock fewer than twenty of us, all told, went in.

Although the door was unlocked and the air conditioner was functioning, no lights were on. While John turned

---

The Rev. Virginia Barksdale is in a joint ministry with her husband in Presbyterian churches in Madison and Gordonsville, Virginia. She is a graduate of Southwestern University at Memphis and Presbyterian School of Christian Education, and she has an M.L.S. from George Peabody College for Teachers. Ms. Barksdale and her husband were missionaries in Japan for sixteen years. She was ordained in the Presbyterian Church in the U.S. after serving the church described in this chapter for three years as a lay minister.

through the pulpit Bible, it became clear that the organist was not on hand. Little conferences were held in loud whispers, and soon everybody was looking at me. Someone opened the instrument, someone else plugged it in, and another person handed me the hymnbook. I clicked the switch, and nothing happened. One more expert came tiptoeing up, whispering instructions. We held the button down, waited sixty interminable seconds, and finally got a note to play. Almost half of those present had been involved in this emergency. Now they all sat down and became the congregation.

That is how it is in a small church, especially when it has been without a leader for a long time. Erin had said she could not play for the service that day, but who was responsible to find a replacement? At the organ I do only in a pinch, but a small church has lots of pinches.

Soon it was my Sunday to preach, and a congregational meeting was called. The chairperson of the nominating committee said, "If anyone has any objection to having a woman for a minister, please stand up and say what it is."

No one stood, and no negative votes were recorded, but of course that did not mean unanimous acceptance or enthusiasm for this new venture. They had had retired ministers, and one with a mid-career crisis; now they were down to a woman. They were resigned.

On the other hand, I was exhilarated!

Appropriate committees were soon at work to legalize the relationship. I seemed to be the answer for this little church that had been without a pastor for more than a year. The trouble was, I was not ordained. My master's degree was from Presbyterian School of Christian Education in Richmond, Virginia. I had taken many of my courses at Union Seminary across the street, but in 1951, when I graduated, they were not granting degrees to women. Preachers were men.

So I was installed as a lay minister with a three-year commission to preach in Maxwell Church. Official restrictions were added: I must have a male member of the congregation assist in worship each Sunday morning, and I was to preach in a robe. Fair enough. I found a choir robe that was acceptable.

Even a large church begins to show some strain if the time between pastors is extended. In small churches lay people are particularly unsure of their skills in areas such as leading worship, teaching classes, and putting together a weekly bulletin. Few are there to share the load. Inevitably, some stitches get dropped. Attendance falls, and the dreaded downward spiral begins. As numbers decline, so does morale, and so does budget. The voices of the faithful few begin to echo in an almost empty sanctuary.

Long before I got there, Sunday school had ceased to meet. Two preschoolers, one first grader, one sixth grader, and three teens were our congregation's only children and youth. To get started, we put everyone over ten years old in one class. Drama, art, music, creative writing, interviewing, puppets, and even a little rudimentary dance were used before the year was out. Proper Miss Vivian, with white hair and silk dress, added a garland of fig leaves for her role as Eve. Noah and his wife came in boots and slickers on their day to lead. Joseph got a modern setting in a short story called "Cowboy Joe." Every Monday morning volunteers for the next Sunday met for a brainstorming session. We scrambled the rest of the week to get it together in time, and almost always it clicked. Sunday schools have done worse.

The Christian education program was a good place to begin. It afforded the pastor opportunity for concentrated work with many small groups responsible for planning and leadership. It involved everyone, offering each a chance to use his or her talents. It gave us intimate, informal contacts. I had training and assurance in Christian education and recognized that this approach was working well, and it was important to do something very well, very soon, because image building was a high priority. Small churches often think of themselves as mediocre, almost nonviable. A successful program in a small church must do what the small church does best—develop persons. Like many women who are fine-tuned to the need to encourage, I had helped my own children do what they could do and stretch toward the next goal. The same sort of nurturing is involved in the kind of program building I used.

In fact, many skills and sensitivities traditionally associated with a woman's place in the home and family are extremely useful in a small church. Maxwell Church was the child who had not made the team. Its attempts to do better were frustrated by equipment too heavy to handle. The Sunday school literature was written for large classes, and most pastoral leadership was beyond the power of a small church to attract. For a while, a sympathetic, loving, even protective approach was needed. Maxwell Church needed to play in a league where they could shine, and it was my responsibility to lift up and celebrate the excellences at hand. Women are accustomed to this role in families.

Meanwhile, two wonderful teachers were meeting week after week with a class of one and a class of two. So when three adults asked for a Sunday evening class, how could I refuse because the numbers were small? I was learning the significance of giving one's best, whether to a class of two or one of two dozen. As that vision took shape in me, it took shape in every class. Our few children were a *precious* few. It is far easier to meet the needs of one or two than of many, and that was a strength we celebrated.

Winter was coming on that first year. I heard of some prospects in a little country house and found a young mother with two children and a background hard to believe. Sheila had revolted against her Presbyterian upbringing and had become part of the hippie world. She was married, divorced, went through college, was married and divorced again. "I can't come to your church," she said. "I don't have a dress."

"I don't care," I told her, "and the Lord doesn't care. Do you mind what anyone else thinks?"

The next Sunday was winter's worst. When she walked into Sunday school in her jeans, two other chilly ladies were wearing pants, for the first time ever. In our free-wheeling class, she was able to say, "I left all this a long time ago and went another way, but I'm glad you have kept the church going and have the Sunday school here for my boys."

We *loved* her. Her faith was too immediate and personal, her convictions too blazing for comfort, and once in a while she was wrong. Still, having her was a constant challenge to our professions of faith, and by and large it was a challenge we met. Maxwell Church put its arms around these three, tried to understand, tried to help, tried not to judge or lose patience. Somehow we knew they were God's gift to us; the truth of God was happening in our love toward them.

Let me be honest. Sheila was teaching a class, singing in the choir, and heading the hunger fund—we had every reason to appreciate her. But we might have offered an icy welcome on that icy morning and turned her away.

The scenario might also have been different if the minister had been a man, for Sheila's relationships with men had never worked out well. Her husband had beaten her, and a policeman refused to help when she asked. A little of her indignation over the way the world is weighted in favor of the masculine I could share from my experience, but there was no sexual dimension in the caring I offered. Besides, as a woman in a role traditionally filled by men, I was a model of respectability and success to which she could relate.

By spring our intergenerational class was a burden to maintain. The teens had brought some friends and deserved a class of their own. The adults ordered their own material and found a teacher. I took on the lone sixth grader for a "Tuesday school" since I could not handle any more on Sunday. On the second Tuesday, as Ross and I strolled down to the river for a box of sand, two neighborhood ragamuffins tagged along. Then they came in to help turn it into Moses's wilderness, and lo, we had recruited two more faithful.

These children were really dirty and tousled. Their father was said to be an alcoholic, and the mother, with seven children to support, could not even keep up with meals and laundry. The teacher of our first grader called me with the rumor that they had lice and might infect us. When I phoned the doctor, he offered free treatment if necessary. So with some degree of reluctance Maxwell Church put its arms around two more. It taxed our tact to find ways to help them, but even when they came munching crackers and dropped crumbs on the lovely carpeted parlor, every adult tried to find something about them to compliment.

One had a sweet voice, so soon there was a junior choir that performed monthly, featuring Maud's talent at every opportunity. Both had pretty faces, and our ex-beautician recognized the possibilities in their long hair. She asked permission from their parents to "play with it," and so it happened one dreary afternoon that children, pastor, beautician, shampoo, hair dryer, rollers, barrettes—the works—assembled in the church kitchen, and a little miracle took place. Cinderellas turned into princesses; the mirror confirmed it. Light from their faces brightened the whole block as we stood in the kitchen door and watched them whirl down the street together, smiling and speaking to everyone in sight. A holy thing happened, sacrament unbidden, the Washing of the Hair.

It was a motherly little ministry we performed, the beautician and I. It was her ministry, actually, but I think it happened because she knew her pastor would understand it, value it, and enjoy being part of it.

In a small church it is fairly easy to tailor the ministry to the need. Committees could meet for years and plan programs that would not meet a specific need as exactly as the Washing of the Hair. Or sending the hometown newspaper to a senior citizen who had gone to live with his son. Or getting Lucy's clothes to the laundromat on snowy days when she could not make it safely with her cane. We work with people more than with causes. The more clearly the needs are seen, the more nearly they can be met. And it is easier to see in a smaller setting. Poverty was not a statistic at Maxwell; it was two little girls.

This enormous plus in smaller churches is sometimes seen as a minus by church officials who look in dismay at our annual reports. "What have you done for your community?" they want to know. "Why not sponsor a day care center? Organize a hunger walk? Set up Meals on Wheels?"

At some points it is important—and possible—to organize for ministry, widen vision, and meet some of the challenges set before us by the staff of our denominational headquarters. But marvelous, effective ministry can take place under less grandiose labels. Since more than half the congregations in mainline Protestant denominations have fewer than two hundred members, the homely realities of caring for people in small numbers and modest circumstances need to enter the picture more often.

When my vacation came, the pulpit was filled by laymen from the area. This was less expensive than finding ministers and paying mileage. I did not object because I reasoned that my sermons would compare favorably and there would be an appreciative welcome back. As it happened, most people just stayed away from worship during that time and had to be recruited again in the fall. Some smaller churches fail to appreciate the value of professional education for preaching, so the inclination to protect the budget needs to be resisted strongly at this point.

Some of this attitude stems from the low-image syndrome. Helping the church feel worth the time of the experts is part of the job. Another part is getting the experts to experience smallness again, to remember that great people live in small places and stand as ready to respond to appropriate leadership as anyone else. A woman can use her natural visibility in the ministry to champion the smaller church. With unaccustomed boldness I now ask only for the best— best mission speakers, best music, best preachers.

People in small churches often have wonderful skills and abilities, but not always with words. Don't tell Maxwell Church to *prioritize*, or *dimensionalize*. To many of its members, such language communicates nothing, but in no sense does that mean they lack intelligence. Old farmer Frank is giving his wife diamonds for every special occasion this year. He had both the knowledge and the cash to buy them at the right time as a hedge against inflation. In his work, abstract jargon is no asset, and he has succeeded handsomely without it.

Preaching to these people is quite as great a challenge as preaching to a thousand-member congregation. The task is finding that fine line that does not insult intelligence, on the one hand, and does not get too bookish on the other. It is no use to exhort them to worship Jesus Christ as Lord. Rather, show Christ to them in his struggling humanity—asking for guidance, moving in obedience, reaching for power, winning our victory, shining alive in resurrection.

It has been said that in small churches the pastoral function is most important. My experience has been that to a significant degree that function is carried out from the pulpit. A sermon is worth the hours it takes to get the great truths into specifics. In this kind of preaching women seem to excel. Again, this strength can be traced to the traditional role, for women have long dealt with the nitty gritty. Their life-stuff daily demonstrates that religion expresses itself in the midst of a hundred humble responsibilities, or it fails to express itself at all. Jesus' humble life baptizes the ordinary. It demands telling—singing forth—in ordinary words for ordinary hearers. People are hungry to hear *gospel*. Where it is preached, strength, caring, and joy begin to develop. Believers begin to accept their own proper priesthood and serve one another. So the pastoral ministry is multiplied from the pulpit.

At Maxwell elders and deacons were on the rotary system, with one year of ineligibility between three-year terms. There were six on each board. Officers had long been chosen more for honor than for leadership, but it did not matter; their business had been mainly to rubberstamp the minister's plans.

The church was quite willing to adopt a unicameral system. We did it on the line of least resistance—giving the six deacons a measure of preparation and ordaining them all elders. Twelve elders were far too many for Maxwell, but the congregation wanted to keep that number.

We established six committees, with two elders and several other members of the congregation on each. The chairperson was always an elder. Elders were willing to be named chairpersons, but they were reluctant to select committee members or call meetings until I established dates, set agendas, and met with them for a year or so. Actually, they had to learn what an education committee or outreach committee was responsible for. I wrote careful job descriptions.

On some committees the chairperson was clearly the least equipped to lead. This was awkward, almost painful, but we just struggled and tried to work around it. The person felt inadequate enough without our adding to the burden. The committee members and I only encouraged, thanked, and tried to pick up the pieces. We had long survived inadequate planning, sloppy follow-through, and total lack of evaluation. Program in a smaller church has to be second to people. People are immediate and real. Program is fiction, a drama to tell us somebody else's truth in a place away from us. The people are our own local truth. Offend, discourage, hurt them, and what is accomplished for some distant person or cause is negated by the effect on the one at hand. At Maxwell, knowing the rotation would change things next year, we could wait it out.

Sometimes I forced a committee to make choices by putting two or three possibilities before them and flatly refusing to show a preference. They had to experience holding the power before they could really take responsibility. But how they grew! A worship committee that once trembled to fill the pulpit in my absence planned World Communion Sunday with international students for guests. The Brazilian's accent was hard to understand. The Oriental was shy. But the Nigerian brought his date, a young black woman from our community, and all were entertained for lunch in the home of one of our elders. The Nigerian announced that his father was a polygamist, and some real dialogue ensued. It is a picture to cherish—our elder seating and serving such an assortment in his own dining room. I could never have persuaded him to do such a thing. The committee planned it.

The first year had some rugged spots. I lacked some skills. How do you get cooperation from officers? Upgrade the music? Assert yourself against the traditional lighted Christmas tree beside the pulpit? How do you investigate a transient? Handle your grief enough to lead the funeral? I longed for seminary training, but other ministers kept telling me, "That's not what you learn in seminary."

Then there was the rough spot with the young adults.

Where were they, the strength and future of the church? What could we over-thirties do to get them back? These were the lost sheep of the house of Israel, so to speak, sons and daughters of the congregation who had become bored and disenchanted and now were busy with other things. No amount of visiting brought results, so we sent invitations to a dinner, planned a fine program, provided a baby sitter, and had a great evening, which resulted in plans to continue. Attendance went from twenty-five to fourteen to four, and in six weeks all was off.

Another rough spot was a personal relationship gone drastically askew. When Ted tickled me during a fellowship supper, my kneejerk reaction was a taut, "Stop that!" that swiveled every head in the kitchen. Some weeks later there was another incident. After a difficult meeting he called to announce, "What you did at the session meeting last night was unforgivable."

Although Ted had joined the church during my ministry, he never really accepted it. He moved from a town where he was a person of stature and was surprised that his reputation did not move with him. His influence on the session was usually negative. And in the end there is no sweet victory to report; he left us. Maxwell Church moved more smoothly with Ted out, but his departure represented my failure, and it was with real sorrow that I saw him go. There were pressures on Ted that had to do with retirement. He saw my less-than-minimum salary as extravagant "for a woman." But the last straw was my bearded college-student son.

Women serving as pastors are very likely to encounter a male ego that cannot accept a woman in a position of authority. The tickling episode may have been an unconscious attempt to turn me into a girl. To my surprise most of the congregation supported me, and even the others recognized the difficulty. There are no neutrals on this kind of question, and no one in the dark. The famous fishbowl effect of a small town was in full force.

Both Ted and I had to shake off the dust from our feet and go on. This is particularly painful in a small church, where it is so important to keep the group together.

Another awkward spot was having my husband moderate the session. His work was thirty miles away. He knew the church, but he did not know its business. That arrangement was becoming a charade.

Not being able to perform the sacraments meant I missed the high moments and celebrations. When I had trained new officers for three months, it was absurd to withdraw for John to ordain them. I could not even join the other officers in the laying on of hands.

After a year, at the request of the session, I asked the presbytery to ordain me under the "Extraordinary Clause." This means that "only the formal educational requirements may be waived and an assignment in exegesis substituted which does not require knowledge of the original languages."[2] The presbytery accepted me as a candidate, and the requirements—theological thesis, standard examinations, sermon before the presbytery—engaged my study time for the next year.

Several members of the congregation became staunch supporters in this endeavor. Our teachers understood the work that was going into it, and at each test I passed even our ragamuffin children expressed their pride. It was a warm surprise to discover their caring response.

That summer a new young couple moved to town and found us. We were trying a vacation church school, and Sue did a spectacular job with the junior class. Spence's bass made all the difference to the choir, and when baby Sal joined the world, we all tried to be grandparents. It was lonesome for them in our little town, though, because most people had lived there forever and had a settled circle of friends. Eventually another new young couple moved in across the street from Sue and Spence. Soon they were playing bridge together, then coming to church together. Other couples were gradually attracted to the group. They picked a mission project and raised $500. They refurbished the nursery, took kitchen duty for the Christmas party, got a Sunday school class going for themselves. The young adults had come to life on their own, and their impact vitalized every area of the church. It happened because two new families needed some fun. Their children swelled the Sunday school. Every classroom was in use, and some were overflowing.

Finding and claiming these young families was the number one priority for Maxwell Church. When parents of the newcomer couples visited, they thanked me for bringing their children into the active life of the church. I have reflected on this phenomenon as a parent. All of us in Maxwell failed to bring in our own children, but we did succeed with these newcomers—who then succeeded with our children! Something hearty and strong flows in the many-membered body of Christ, growing and building itself up in love.

By this time many in Maxwell had ceased to think of themselves as being "down to a woman." In fact, calling me gave the church a certain pleasant notoriety in the presbytery and surrounding communities. I was often asked to speak—to high school graduating classes, the teachers' professional association, the United Methodist women's group, and on twenty minutes notice to the Rotary Club. I was the token woman on several committees. The church began to be proud of itself for calling a woman and responding so beautifully.

Women in the congregation were a great concern to me. There were so many of them, relatively speaking. They were there before I was—unmarrieds, widows, divorcees, mostly a little older, and a few very old indeed. Perhaps the most agreeable part of my work was visiting these women. Their strength is amazing. I learned how important it is in little churches, in little towns, to keep your relationships straight. If you lose these friends, there is no other circle to turn to, and besides, you keep meeting these people in the grocery store and post office whether you are friendly or not. I learned that in a small church and town only so much candor is wise. Expressing every frustration may produce situations so prickly it takes years to get them unstuck. That is a little of what these women taught me.

Because I was a woman, their relationship with me as minister was free of one unfortunate element: I was not a crutch for them to lean on. They did not depend on me to fix their problems as they might have depended on a man. We were friends who supported each other. Most churches have more women than men, and most women can reach a state of easy honesty with a woman minister.

The question is asked: "Do men come to you with their problems as much as they would to a man?" I have no basis for comparison. Do men go to anybody? I stayed and prayed with Dave in the hospital when Joanne was being operated on. Matthew came day after day to work through his indecision about changing jobs. Paul confessed in shouts and tears that he had wanted to drive off the bridge. And Doris's father-in-law, who has yet to come to church, asked my help in a custody case. The unemployed man and his family who camped by the river came; and the Main Street coffee crowd, all men, took up the family's cause in the back booth of the drug store.

However, the men needed to be protective and had some reluctance to let me work in the church alone after dark. I am far from fearless, but how can a minister do all her work and driving in daylight hours? Something scary may happen sometime, and when it does, I will be afraid. In the meantime it is helpful to set aside as much fear as possible and just do the job.

Churches are uneasy about calling a woman partly because of the unknowns about her relationships to men. Small churches are often in small towns, where a rigid set of expectations controls behavior. A woman minister needs to keep her call clearly in mind, be certain that people understand the theological basis of her joy and freedom among them—joy and freedom she must have to carry out her ministry. The joking and camaraderie natural to people working together can be lightly enjoyed when that is exactly what it is, but the first hint of flirtation will be noticed and resented. Such attitudes are quite unfair, for male ministers use their masculine charm innocently without risk of reprobation. "Little old ladies" are delighted by the attention, and their husbands do not mind. But woe to the woman preacher who uses such an approach to the "little old men." Still, our femininity is part of who we are, and we have to bring our whole selves to this work. Until society grants us the right to go where we are needed, we can avoid gossip when possible though we must risk it when necessary. Once it is thoroughly established that our presence in the community is as a servant of Christ, questions that might be raised in the first year or so of a pastorate do not come up so often.

My ordination, when it finally happened, was a standing-room-only event. Pastor and people had achieved it together and truly celebrated it together. This is not a second-rate way to become an ordained minister. Besides their great gifts of acceptance and encouragement, the congregation marked this high occasion with the presentation of a beautiful pulpit robe. The following Sunday I led a slow procession down the center aisle for it to be admired from every angle.

Often I wished to be part of a staff, with a male minister to take the administration chores and some other responsibilities I do not enjoy. Two multistaff churches within commuting distance of my husband's work did make some job overtures to me, but when it was time to move, family considerations took us in another direction. After almost five years at Maxwell, the roll had reached ninety-nine and attendance was usually in the sixties.

It makes me uncomfortable to claim special virtues for the ministry of women in smaller churches, but women *can* do it well. As a woman of my generation was expected to be wife, mother, hostess, chauffeur, cook, economist, and den mother, so she can be pastor, preacher, counselor, administrator, educator, evangelist, cheerleader, and, in a pinch, organist.

Some of the best people coming out of seminaries now are women. I have a fear that for a while women, even more than men, will need to follow the pattern of onward and upward in order to prove themselves. But I also have a hope that some of those women may find themselves so fulfilled and rewarded as the nurturer of an intimate congregation that they will stay, because it is just where they want to be.

Notes

1. The name of the church and the names of the individuals I describe in this chapter are fictitious.

2. *The Book of Church Order of the Presbyterian Church in the United States*, 1974, #27-5.

PREACHING THROUGH METAPHOR

Janice Riggle Huie

"I will sing with the spirit
and I will sing with the mind also."
[1 Cor. 14:15b]

Walking toward the sanctuary on my first Sunday in my new church, I was stopped by a white-haired patriarch of the congregation. Audacious enough to ask what others were too polite to say, he questioned, "I want to know just one thing: Can you preach?"

"Can women preach?" is a central question for both clergywomen and congregations. Local churches are shaped by a long cultural and ecclesiastical tradition that has emphasized that women are persons who respond better than they initiate, who should be seen rather than heard, and

---

The Rev. Janice Riggle Huie is co-pastor, with her husband, of St. Mark United Methodist Church in Austin, Texas. She is a graduate of the University of Texas and Perkins School of Theology. Ms. Huie chairs the Division of Ordained Ministry of the United Methodist Board of Higher Education and Ministry.

who are passive rather than assertive. Therefore, church people rarely assume a woman can effectively proclaim the Word. Morever, few persons have consistently heard women preach; so it's still easy to say of a woman who preaches well, "She's an exception." On the other hand, congregations ordinarily assume the preaching competence of male ministers because the church has long assured its members that they can trust a man to represent faithfully the word of Christ. A woman slowly earns her authority from the congregation as members experience her as someone who can be trusted to tell the truth in word and deed.

For clergywomen, preaching frequently brings to the surface unresolved issues about personal identity and the nature of her faith. With no role models to look to, women frequently question their own potency in the pulpit. Many preachers struggle with questions of authority and self-doubt, but those issues are exacerbated when women have no consistent models of effective preaching by a woman. Without clear images of our own experience as valuable and competent, we fall easy prey to self-depreciation ("I could never preach"), anger ("Nobody would listen to me"), or despair ("Preaching is a lost cause"). Unless she simply wants to copy her male peers, a woman is forced to plumb deeply her own experience. Questions like, "What should I wear in the pulpit? I don't want to look like a man" are often outward signs of the inner struggle, "How can I most effectively communicate the gospel, allowing my experience as a woman to be reflected?"

Furthermore, preaching demands that women struggle daily with Scripture that assumes a patriarchial world view and a God predominately imaged in masculine terms. A woman grapples regularly with texts that assume that she is not quite human, is not capable of speaking publicly, or should defer to a man. Part of my own struggle has been to discover images, biblical and others, that re-present God's nature in more inclusive ways. Do I really believe that I can be an instrument of God's self-revelation? By what criteria do I decide which parts of the Scripture are life-denying traditions and which parts reflect the true nature of God's love? Do I trust myself to interpret the Scriptures creatively? How much am I willing to risk to participate in birthing the inclusive new creation promised in Scripture?

In my own search for adequate methods to communicate the gospel, I have become convinced of the necessity of presenting images of faith that allow the hearers to reframe their experience of the world in the light of God's saving activity. Through the sermon the preacher extends both biblical and contemporary images of God's activity in such a way that people perceive new possibilities for themselves and the world. For example, to present the creation as "groaning in travail" (Rom. 8:22) is to portray the universe in the birth process. The image invites the hearer to understand her or his own pain and suffering as meaningful because it moves in the direction of new life. In March 1980 Bishop Oscar Romero, the outspoken advocate of human rights in El Salvador, was assassinated while he consecrated the host at mass. To present his life and death as a contemporary sign of the Crucified One invites the hearer to put in new perspective what it means for North American Christians to participate in the life and death of Christ.

In their own struggle to develop adequate personal images of the liberating love of God, many women are exploring their own imagination and intuition. As they share their own stories, they are able to perceive God's story in new ways. For example, one Advent I heard a sermon, "Waiting for the Birth of the Christ Child," preached by a clergywoman who was herself "great with child." She described her delight at the baby's first movement, her fears of what might happen in labor and delivery, her own need for love and assurance, and the wonderful mystery that was growing inside of her. The clergywoman's story became a new lens through which I was able to perceive Mary, mother of Jesus, and Mary's faithfulness that ". . . there would be fulfilment of what was spoken to her from the Lord" (Luke 1:45). The preacher's own body pointed to one aspect of the nature of God as she read Isaiah's vision of God's promise to Israel:

"Shall I bring to the birth and not cause to bring forth? . . .
As one whom his mother comforts, so I will comfort you"
(Isa. 66:9, 13).

This determined search for new means of representing
God's love in ways that include the feminine is a gift which
many women bring to the pulpit. We are recovering long-
neglected biblical images which reveal God in feminine
terms. In that process we are discovering the power of our
imaginations to create fresh gospel images and reframe old
ones. We are learning the potency of the story—my story,
God's story, our story—as a way to witness to the vitality of
faith. This use of metaphor, story, and imagination is clearly
a quality which is not confined to women. Rather, it is a gift
of God growing out of the struggle for an inclusive new creation.

In this chapter I wish to invite the reader to explore the
value of metaphorical preaching. By metaphorical preaching
I mean communicating the gospel through the use of story,
image, and poetry. Metaphorical preaching represents both
a recovery of a long-neglected biblical mode of communication and a recovery of imaginative, expressive, symbolic aspects of human experience.

At heart I believe expanded use of metaphor is a feminist
issue. Metaphor holds the possibility of allowing us to break
out of traditional language that has shaped a flat, one-
dimensional understanding of God and fostered an oppres-
sive social context for men as well as women. Metaphor can
enable us to transcend a prosaic style of preaching, which
frequently reduces both men and women to heads without
hearts, minds without spirits. Metaphor is participatory rather than authoritarian. It implies a partnership between
preacher and congregation in which the preachers speak *for*,
with, and *from* the people rather than *to* people. Metaphor
invites the whole people of God to envision and live in the
new creation.

I wish to emphasize that I have no intention of devaluing
or minimizing the importance of a consistent, coherent
framework for sermons. Neither do I wish to demean the
importance of "singing with our minds." Indeed, the church

has never been in greater need of a disciplined intellect in its preachers. Skillful exegetical work, cogent reasoning, and careful theologizing are crucial to faithful preaching. However, I am suggesting that the clergy need to examine their preaching carefully to determine whether their sermons are so cognitive that they implicitly discount the nonrational in human experience. Before discussing specific approaches to metaphorical preaching, I want to delineate some of the problems of a didactic approach to preaching the gospel.

> "Bitzer," said Thomas Gadgrind, "your definition of a horse." "Quadruped. Gramnivorous. Forty teeth, namely twenty-four grinders, four eye-teeth, and twelve incisive. Sheds coat in spring; in marshy countries sheds hoofs too. Hoofs hard, but requiring to be shod with iron. Age known by marks in mouth." Thus (and much more) Bitzer.
> "Now girl number twenty," said Mr. Gadgrind, "you know what a horse is."[1]

The School of Hard Facts over which Mr. Gadgrind presided in Charles Dickens's *Hard Times* was a school of fixed answers. It was a school in which the dictionary definition was perceived as an adequate description for an idea or experience. To classify and explain is "to know what a horse is."

Today, more than a century later, many of us "preach" the gospel as though we had learned well our lessons from Mr. Gadgrind. Our sermons classify and describe. They argue and explain. We preach the gospel as though we were describing a horse to "girl number twenty." Søren Kierkegaard lamented that the gospel has become a "piece of information." Passion is replaced by descriptions of passion. The net effect for the church, he said, can be compared to reading a cookbook to someone who is hungry.[2] The fallacy is assuming that information will bring about transformation.

Having been taught not to trust the spirit of God inside ourselves, we've been timid in expanding upon the literal words of Scripture. Sermons often do a creditable job of explaining a particular Scripture—describing the context, de-

fining the vocabulary, discussing the writer's intent, and
even illustrating a major theme with a contemporary example. Congregations frequently make a valiant attempt at listening, but as a woman in my church noted pointedly one
Sunday morning after I had preached a "teach-y" sermon on
the meaning of covenant, "What you said might be true and
probably is, but so what? What difference does God's covenant make in our society?"

At least three problems are apparent with expository
preaching. First, when preaching is understood as simple explanation of a text, the congregation often experiences more
of a history lesson than an invitation to understand their
own individual and community life in the light of God's salvation story. For example, in Scripture God is compared to a
she-bear, a nursing mother, a mighty warrior, a king, and a
father. The kingdom is compared to a mustard seed growing
into a great tree or seeds planted in various kinds of soil or
leaven kneaded into flour. Judgment is compared to a king
separating the sheep from the goats or a bridegroom arriving and discovering that some of the bridesmaids had oil for
their lamps while others did not. The Scripture uses the ordinary, alive language of the day to tell the salvation story.
Unfortunately, when modern preachers attempt to use those
vibrant first-century metaphors in our cultural context, they
often fall lifeless upon our hearers' ears. Our basic framework of human experience simply does not include kings
and kingdoms, shepherds and sheep, or oil lamps. Most of
us have never seen a mustard seed or kneaded yeast into
flour to make bread. Therefore, the preacher must spend
large portions of a sermon describing and explaining the
biblical metaphors. We learn much about first-century life,
but we're left wondering "what difference it makes." The
urgent question is, "How do I experience the Kingdom or
God's love or judgment *now*?" Too often the congregation is
left holding the dictionary definition of those concepts rather than experiencing the biblical faith in their context.

Furthermore, through years of selective memory the
church has compounded the problem of how best to tell the
biblical story by reducing the number of metaphors to com-

municate God's activity rather than expanding them. For example, in referring to God in sermons and liturgy, preachers frequently use *father, savior, lord,* and *king.* Three of the four are clearly male, and the fourth is perceived as male. Consequently, preachers often present women and men alike with a truncated image of God.

The second problem with didactic or expository preaching is rooted in the basic character of Scripture itself. The Bible is primarily revelation, not persuasion. It is confession, not classification. It is proclamation, not explanation. The reader does not encounter ideas, but a story—the story of the victory of life over death. Amos Wilder notes,

> A Christian can confess his faith wherever he is, and without his Bible, just by telling a story or a series of stories. It is through the Christian story that God speaks, and all heaven and earth come into it. . . . The special character of the stories in the New Testament lies in the fact they are not told for themselves, they are not only about other people, but that they are always about us. They locate us in the very midst of the great story and plot of all time and space, therefore relate us to the great dramatist and storyteller, God.[3]

To understand the primary task of preaching as giving information, explaining doctrine, teaching church school, or doing group therapy is to stand outside the basic framework of faith. Furthermore, it frequently is boring. To preach faithfully is to use the words of human story to tell God's story.

Finally, cognitive, analytical sermons assume that persons are transformed through rational and intellectual means. Didactic sermons appeal to the analyst, the technician, the programmer, and the thinker inside each of us—not to the artist, the dancer, the poet, and the "child" inside each of us. Theologically, we say we believe in the whole person, but our sermons frequently appeal only to the cognitive, analytic aspects of the human being. Modern psychology has demonstrated what Scripture assumes—that the whole person must be involved in transformation. It is not enough to be convinced intellectually of God's love. Preacher and congregation must be able to imagine that they are nurtured by a loving mother/father God.

In his play *Saint Joan*, George Bernard Shaw points to the importance of trusting the imagination in one's encounter with God. Joan's willingness to believe her intuition enables her to speak and act with so much power that she is able to rally demoralized French troops on to victory. In explaining her calling to a skeptical nobleman, Joan reveals where her authority comes from.

> JOAN: I hear voices telling me what to do. They come from God.
> ROBERT: They come from your imagination.
> JOAN: Of course. That is how the messages of God come to us.[4]

Joan understood that listening to the intuitive, creative dimension within herself is to listen to the creative center of the universe. Faith itself requires an imaginative leap; faith in God makes one believe that it is possible to envision the ultimate. To listen to my imagination is to trust that God does indeed speak to me.

Preaching requires that a person be audacious enough to "speak the unspeakable" and "search the unsearchable." Therefore, a preacher must believe that she or he is centered in God and able to perceive God's word. Moreover, we must believe that we are instruments for re-presenting God's truth in such a way that hearers can be transformed by God. We claim our own authority to the extent that we trust our imagination as a way that "the messages of God come to us." To be sure, personal imagination must be tested by the experience of the community of faith. It must be examined in light of the witnesses of the historical community through Scripture and tradition. It must not be illogical or inconsistent. Our words in the pulpit and our actions in the parish must be congruent in order for us to be believed by our congregations. Nonetheless, trusting the mystery and wonder of our own imaginations draws us closer to trusting the mystery and wonder of God.

Sallie McFague notes, "There are not explicit statements about God; everything is refracted through earthly metaphor or story. Metaphor is . . . the heart . . . of religious reflection."[5] A preacher points to the Mysterious One by telling the congregation what the experience of God is *like*. We tell the congregation what judgment and grace are *like*. We tell a story about what God's love is *like*.

In metaphorical preaching ordinary life and transcendent life are woven together with such care that there is no way to separate them without tearing the fabric. Day-to-day living becomes a window through which we get a glimpse of life eternal. The eternal illuminates and gives focus to the daily. To attempt dividing the transcendent from the ordinary is to blur our vision of both.

Preaching metaphorically is like telling a fairy story. As in fairy tales, one involves the hearers by telling a simple tale in plain language that allows them to look in on a deeper reality and discover themselves. The art of preaching the gospel is never simply cognitive or rational; rather, it invites us to enter a new world which we cannot completely define. J. R. R. Tolkien, the modern writer of fairy stories, notes, "Faerie cannot be caught in a net of words; for it is one of its qualities to be indescribable, though not imperceptible. It has many ingredients, but analysis will not necessarily discover the secret of the whole."[6]

From the point of view of the congregation, imaginative preaching of the gospel of Jesus Christ presents a vision of the new creation in which members are invited to participate. It is like watching a play and at the end discovering oneself in the leading role. It is like dreaming a vivid dream in which the hearers are exploring some new possibility. Upon waking up, they realize that they really can be what they dreamed of being. In metaphorical sermons the preacher takes a single object, puts it under a microscope, and invites the congregation to discover new wonderful shapes and colors and depths.

Imaginative preaching has several distinct advantages over a more didactic, prosaic style. Imaginative preaching derives its power from appealing to the creative, intuitive dimension within each person. A yearning for mystery and transcendence is part of our humanity, but it is an aspect which has been grossly overlooked in our technological society built on complex, logical systems. For example, a person programming a computer all day is not eager for more data. A student attempting to absorb page after page of information is not excited to hear another lecture. A manager who has spent the week trying to persuade and convince is not anticipating with delight a one-way conversation in which a preacher details what to do. People are hungry for the poetic, intuitive, spontaneous qualities of life. There is a longing to be in touch with feelings and dreams, a desire for mystery and the transcendent. A preacher can use the sermon as an opportunity to offer people the same thing that Jesus did, a vision of a new creation—a new heaven and a new earth and the assurance that the new creation has already come in the Christ event and is unfolding in their lives.

Imaginative preaching appeals to the whole congregation, not just adults. Children are just as much involved in imaginative story-preaching as adults. Indeed, the involvement of children can even lead adults to forget their own sophistication for a few minutes and to "overhear" a story intended for children. The current popularity of "children's sermons" may stem partially from the reality that children's sermons are frequently learning experiences for adults as well. I believe that "children's dialogues" can have significant value for children, but they also can drive a wedge further between the human need for play and spontaneity and the need for careful structure and logic. An imaginative sermon, however, communicates both to children and to the child inside each of us. If we really believe that children are a valued part of the body of Christ, then preachers must be willing to move toward a sermon style that includes them.

Imaginative preaching relates the human story, my story, the congregation's story, and God's story in specific ways. The congregation goes home with specific instances which are rooted in their experience rather than an abstract concept which usually evaporates at the church door. For example, each year our congregation celebrates All Saints Day, during which we recall the lives of our mothers and fathers in the faith. For several years I had preached sermons that sought to explain how God is working in history through the lives of people. However, All Saints Day came alive the Sunday that I simply told two stories, one about Catherine of Siena, a fourteenth-century saint, and another about Forest Campbell, a greatly loved saint in our congregation. I let the congregation draw their own conclusions about how people's faith in God involves them in the life of the community. The relationship between God's story and the human story was specific and believable because it came out of the experience of the congregation.

Because imaginative preaching is confessional preaching, it is also more passionate. The preacher is not simply giving information, but expressing who she or he is. Since metaphorical preaching seeks to weave together God's story, the congregation's story, and the sermon story, the sermon is also a statement of faith of the preacher. Timid, beginning preachers can communicate convincingly, and manuscript preachers can more easily leave their scripts because they are telling a story of something that they themselves have experienced. Consequently, imaginative preaching is believable and convincing. A passionate preacher is a genuine artist, whose message is "flesh of his [sic] flesh and blood of his [sic] blood."[7]

The simplest form of metaphorical preaching is a storytelling: "In the beginning, God . . ." or "There was once a man who had two sons . . ." or "The reign of God is like ten maidens." The story can be autobiographical, or it can be a recounting of someone else's experience. It might be a fantasy or dream. What is important is that the story illuminate one or more of the levels of meaning in a particular biblical text. It should suggest the same reality as the text, thereby offering the listener another window through which to view that reality.

Well-told stories are characterized by their open-ended style. By that I mean they don't moralize or draw conclusions but allow the imagination of the listener to complete the meaning. They announce good news and invite the hearer to respond. Well-told stories do not end with, "The point of the story is. . . ." Rather, they ignite the imagination of the hearers and call forth from them an imaginative leap. Interesting stories utilize dialogue to express the action so that the characters in the story rather than the narrator tell the listener what is happening. The preacher-storyteller cultivates vivid images or phrases, enabling the listener to see, taste, touch, smell, and hear the action.

For example, Mark frequently uses healing stories to proclaim his belief that Jesus is the Holy One of God. He records,

> And a leper came to him [Jesus] beseeching him, and kneeling said to him. "If you will, you can make me clean." Moved with pity, he stretched out his hand and touched him, and said to him, "I will; be clean." And immediately, the leprosy left him, and he was made clean.   [Mark 1:40–42]

There is initiation and response, speaking and listening. The wording is lean, yet the reader can clearly visualize the scene. Mark makes no attempt to explain the healing or to convince the reader that it "really happened." Rather, he points to a mystery and claims it for the Holy One. Mark stimulates the reader's imagination and invites response.

Barbara Troxell makes use of this narrative style in a sermon on responding to the call of God. She lives in California, the apricot-producing region of the United States.

> Some years ago, in Santa Clara County, California, a family owned an orchard—one of many once filling this fertile valley—now sadly overrun by developers. The family had hundreds of acres of fruit trees, and employed numerous workers.
>
> One day when the apricot crop was at its peak, additional help was needed. The owner asked his sons, who were learning the business, to go out into the orchard and help with the picking of apricots. The first son, when asked, said a quick and enthusias-

tic "Yes." Then he sat around, found more interesting things to do, and never went out of the office into the orchard.

The second son, when the father had earlier asked, said, flatly: "No, I won't go. It's awfully hot out there, and I'm no good at manual labor. I'd rather work on the books. No, father, I don't feel like picking cots."

Later, after thinking it over, realizing that bushels would be lost, and hearing inwardly the urgency of his father's request, the young man changed his mind, turned, went, and worked.

And Jesus said, "Which one did the will of one who asked?"[8]

A second form of metaphorical preaching occurs when the preacher focuses on a particular reality and looks at it from different points of view. For example, Matthew recalls many images that Jesus used to describe the reign of God. It is like a "mustard seed," or "a treasure hidden in a field," or "a merchant in search of fine pearls." No one viewpoint claims that it discloses the whole reality; rather, each analogy or contrast allows the listener to perceive the reality from a different perspective.

A third kind of metaphorical preaching is poetry. It is also highly personal, deeply engaging, and rarely used in contemporory preaching. However, the Hebrew psalmists and prophets found it an effective form of communication.

> Whither shall I go from thy Spirit?
>   Or whither shall I flee from thy presence?
> If I ascend to heaven, thou art there.
>   If I make my bed in Sheol, thou art there!
> If I take the wings of the morning
>   and dwell in the uttermost parts of the sea,
> even there thy hand shall lead me,
>   and thy right hand shall hold me.
>   [Ps. 139:7–10]

McFague notes that the test of a Christian poet is whether the reality with which the poet is dealing is the transformation of the ordinary by the graciousness of God. Genuine Christian poets rely on untranslatable root metaphors which are located in the images, symbols, stories in Scripture.[9]

While poetry is not one of our customary preaching modes, I think it can be a vital one. It can be incorporated into a sermon, or it might be the whole sermon. To be effective, poetry in preaching must take one or more of the root metaphors and place them in a new context, thereby illuminating both the image and the context. Focusing on a particular image in poetic form can be used, as I used it in a sermon on baptism, to help people sense the variety of meanings that water communicates in this sacrament.

> Look at the waters of life.
> You were nurtured
> in the waters of your mother's womb.
> In breaking forth from those waters
> you breathed life.
>
> Baptism.
>
> Touch the waters of life.
> Summer day, long walk,
> Sweat trickling down your back.
> Tired, thirsty, exhausted.
> Cool, clear water
> splashing over head, face, hands.
> Refreshment, renewal, restoration.
>
> Baptism.
>
> Drink deeply of the waters of life.
> Nourishing gardens, birthing forests,
> feeding farm and city.
> Replenishing rivers and sea.
>
> Baptism.
>
> Feel the power of the waters of life.
> Intense energy in a waterfall,
> thunder of breaking waves,
> quiet strength of river shaping granite.
>
> Baptism.

Sense the continuity of the waters of life.
Older than Eve,
covering the earth,
falling as tears
sparkling as a dewdrop
pulsing through our bodies.

Baptism.

Embrace the mystery of water.
Masquerading as soft fog,
hiding as a tiny snowflake,
freezing as ice,
pouring down as rain,
running deep below the surface.

Baptism

Plunge deeply into the waters of life.
Come up fresh and pure.
Remember your baptism.

Be thankful.[10]

A fourth kind of preaching is autobiographical. Beginning with Paul, many of the great preachers have told their personal stories as a metaphor through which to enable others to view the gospel.

> Last of all, as to one untimely born, he appeared also to me. For I am the least of the apostles, unfit to be called an apostle, because I persecuted the church of God. But by the grace of God I am what I am, and his grace toward me was not in vain. On the contrary, I worked harder than any of them, though it was not I, but the grace of God which is with me. Whether then it was I or they, so we preach and so you believed.
>
> [1 Cor. 15:8–11]

The story may be a simple recounting of an actual experience in which the preacher arrives at a new perception of the world because of his or her encounter with another human being. The autobiographical statement may also be a fantasy or a dream in which the preacher realizes God's activity in a new way.

My congregation knows that I enjoy gardening, and I used the following autobiographical fantasy as a way to point to giving and receiving at the heart of life:

The Rosebush

One of the first things I saw when we moved into the parsonage was the rosebush. She was in front of the house almost in the shadow of some overbearing pyracantha bushes. Carpet grass knotted around her three big joints. Black fungus dotted her bottom leaves. Even then she bore a rose for me.

The first year we were so busy around the church that all I had time to do was to pull back the grass from her roots and water her. Even so, I noticed that one day she seemed to smile. Every now and then there would be a tiny bud that would swell and swell until it burst. The petals would carefully unfold, each one savoring its moment of opening to the light. I came every day when the rosebush was making a new blossom. When I cut the almost-open rose and carried it inside, I knew the rosebush gave herself gladly to me.

Our son Matt was born the second year, and my friend fared little better. I did feed her once, and she responded with enough delicate coral roses to fill my best crystal pitcher. I thanked her.

The third year was a big year for roses. With a grubbing hoe and much sweat I hacked out a rose bed on either side of my friend. She would have sisters of different shades and varieties. Bob cut back the pyracantha bushes. I brought in new soil, mulch, and fungicide. Quite unintentionally, I also overindulged the rosebush on fertilizer. After three or four big belches which she discretely disguised as roses the size of small cabbages, we settled back to our comfortable routine. I came to visit her almost every day; now and then she surprised me with a rose.

Spring pretended to come early this year. In great eagerness my friend put out tiny new shoots before any of her sisters did. She wanted to be the first one with a tiny bud for me. Then winter imposed himself again with brutal force, and when I went to see how my friend had fared, I discovered her standing icy and wounded by the wall of the house. Within three days the delicate shoots crumbled like aged paper between my fingers. Not even the sun could make her smile, and I thought she would die.

Slowly, slowly she revived, cautiously sending out new shoots. She would not be the first to blossom this year. I noted that the new leaves were on only one of her branches. The other two reached stiffly upward like naked, atrophied arms.

My friend still smiles at me when I stop by, and I return the favor. Our smiles are tinged with sadness for we both know that this spring and summer will probably be her last. She's spending her remaining strength on this year's roses, and they are all the more precious to me. I'll receive these holy gifts tenderly, joyfully.

Imaginative preaching is not without risk. When the preacher allows the hearers to draw their own conclusions, the congregation might hear a different point than the preacher intended. Furthermore, congregations that have become accustomed to thinking of themselves as empty vessels into which they expect the preacher to pour the word of God may experience frustration at being asked to become involved in the sermon. Preachers who are used to being in control of the hearers may find it difficult not to tell the congregation what they should think. Nonetheless, I believe metaphorical preaching is an effective means of opening our spirit to the direction of God's spirit. As Dom Helder Camara, poet-priest, notes,

Hope without risk
is not hope,
which is believing
in risky loving,
trusting others
in the dark,
the blind leap
letting God take over.[11]

Notes

1. Cited in John Ciardi, *How Does A Poem Mean?* (New York: Houghton Mifflin, 1959), p. 665.

2. Cited in Fred Craddock, *Overhearing the Gospel* (Nashville: Abingdon Press, 1978), p. 28.

3. Amos Wilder, *The Language of the Gospel* (New York: Harper & Row, 1964), pp. 64–65.

4. George Bernard Shaw, *Saint Joan* (London: Constable and Company, 1924), p. 11.

5. Sallie McFague TeSelle, *Speaking in Parables: A Study in Metaphor and Theology* (Philadelphia: Fortress Press, 1975), p. 16.

6. J. R. R. Tolkien, *Tree and Leaf* (London: Unwin Books, 1964), p. 16.

7. Dom Helder Camara, *The Desert Is Fertile* (Maryknoll, N.Y.: Orbis Books, 1974), p. 67.

8. Helen Gray Crotwell, ed., *Women and the Word* (Philadelphia: Fortress Press, 1978), p. 26.

9. TeSelle, *Speaking in Parables*, p. 97.

10. Some of the images in this sermon are drawn from *alive now!* (published by *The Upper Room*), Jan.–Feb., 1979.

11. Camara, *The Desert Is Fertile*, p. 10.

PREACHING IN THE BLACK TRADITION

Leontine T. C. Kelly

I grew up listening to great preaching.

One of eight children born in a Methodist parsonage to David and Ila Turpeau, I had the opportunity to listen weekly to the illustrative story-preaching of my father and to spend several summers with my evangelistic, "walk-about" preaching brother DeWitt. I was not aware at the time that the style, the tone, the substance and purpose of their sermons were patterned in what is now recognizably "the black tradition."

The interpretation of the Word was delivered not only as

The Rev. Leontine T. C. Kelly is pastor of Asbury–Church Hill United Methodist Church in Richmond, Virginia. She is a graduate of Virginia Union University and Union Theological Seminary in Richmond. Ms. Kelly entered the ordained ministry after several years of public school teaching. She has also served as associate director of the Virginia Conference (United Methodist) Council on Ministries.

the story of God's activity in the world through a particular people—the Hebrews—but as the particular Word of God to a people in need of affirmation, the American Negro. The Exodus event of the Hebrew tradition was the continuing frame of reference for God's caring and deliverance of black people from the legal enslavement of the race and the resultant racism. The weekly exhortation was designed to inspire, to give hope, and to declare the eternal watchfulness of a God who never slept.

Isaiah's prophetic word to the Babylonian captives bridged the centuries with assuring hope:

> Have you not known? Have you not heard?
> The LORD is the *everlasting* God,
>   the *Creator* of the ends of the earth.
> He does not faint or grow weary,
>   his understanding is unsearchable.
> He gives *power* to the faint,
>   and to him who has no might he *increases strength.*
> Even youths shall faint and be weary,
>   and young men shall fall exhausted;
> but they who *wait* for the LORD shall renew their
>   strength,
>   they shall mount up with wings like eagles,
> they shall run and not be weary,
>   they shall walk and not faint.
>
> [Isa. 40:28–31, italics added]

The purpose of black preaching was to give definition to the life of a "waiting people." I listened from childhood to outstanding black preacher-leaders as they brought balance between heaven-orientation and earth-bound reality. We were reminded that "justice goes forth perverted" and the "vision awaits its time; it hastens to the end—it will not lie" (Hab. 2:3). We were assured of ways by which the righteous would live by faith and wait. There was no doubt in my young mind that waiting was not sleeping and that we were among the righteous.

I recall packed churches, schools, and civic auditoriums filled with people who traveled miles to hear the late Dr.

Roscoe Conklin Simmons, a preacher and orator; Bishop Lorenzo King of the Methodist Episcopal Church; and, later, Baptist preachers such as Dr. Vernon Johns, a pastor from Charleston, West Virginia; Dr. Mordecai Johnson, president of Howard University; and Dr. Benjamin Mays, president of Morehouse College in Atlanta. I have never forgotten Dr. Mays's sermon on the Scripture, "Thou art weighed in the balances and found wanting" (Dan. 5:27, KJV), or the intense concentration required to follow the complex spiritual journey and genius of Dr. Howard Thurman.

Denomination was of little concern to our community. We were all in the same boat. People from all denominations gathered hungry to hear the Word of the Lord authenticated by the presence and power of the Holy Spirit.

I recall the break in traditional preaching patterns when we had the opportunity to hear the great Marcus Garvey speak. The streets of Cincinnati were lined with crowds of people as the parade moved slowly down Central Avenue on that hot Sunday afternoon. Throngs gathered to witness the black man in black hat with white plumes and his followers of all ages. My younger brother and I watched in awe. He suggested royalty to us, and the stern set of his jaw emphasized the severity of his mission.

The other children would never believe my brother and me when we pointed out the lady dressed in white satin, riding on a white horse, as our Aunt Mamie. In the movement and to the press she was "Madam DeMeana," a top official in the Garvey organization. They thought we were fantasizing. She was, however, my father's sister, and through her we were admitted to a Garvey meeting. I recall the preaching tone that brought fear to my heart. There was no rest moment of consolation. We were alienated in this strange land because we were aliens; we had no business here. God did not intend for us to be here. He would want us to return to our native land, Africa. Marcus Garvey had the plan, the ship, the call from Moses to lead his people back home.

Conversation around the parsonage dinner table included other preachers, visiting and local. We were always included; it was a part of our education. Any movement or event affecting our lives found its way into the Sunday sermons. The sermon happened as the result of and in the midst of the life of the people who not only heard but responded. Crescendos of preparatory prayer and praise. Encouraging "Amen!" Fearful "Lord, have mercy!" Affirming "Preach the Word!" "That's all right!" and "Take your time!" from uninhibited voices. Time was forgotten. No time more important. The preacher finished when he got "there," and "there" was recognized by both proclaimer and listener to demand commitment by the power of the Holy Spirit. "There" was the sustained upward note that held the congregation in a spiritual grip only surrender to God could release.

Despite individual style, black preaching was exciting interpretation of God's Word, dramatically clarified and inspirationally applicable to the need of a people to press on, make their mark, claim their inheritance, prove their God. Anything else was "preaching like a white man."

From this background, so significantly a part of my own faith development, I gained a respect for communicating the Word through preaching.

When my father heard me speak as a teenager (president of the Greater Cincinnati Girl Reserves, which preceded the YWCA's Y-Teens), he commended me. He warned me, however, with the words, "Girl, you keep still when you speak; you are trying to preach!" That was clearly something I was not supposed to do as a female. When the late Bishop Matthew W. Clair, Sr., became a bishop of the Methodist Episcopal Church, one of his first acts was to baptize me. I was three months old. I have been told again and again that he said, "Oh, how I wish you were a boy so that my mantle could fall on you!"

Years later I married a Methodist minister and profound preacher, James David Kelly. He encouraged me to use my native ability to speak and to become a lay speaker in the church. It was in this capacity that I was asked, after my husband's death in 1969, to assume the leadership of his church, Galilee United Methodist, in Edwardsville, Virginia. I accepted with the traditional famous last words, "until you can get somebody!" I was a public school teacher, and I loved my work. The classroom was my particular calling.

Within the year following David's death, I taught a course on "The Inner Life" at the Virginia Conference School of Christian Mission and there felt and responded to my own personal call to the ministry of Jesus Christ. For me the journey toward ordination was a pinnacle experience: It was as if every experience I had ever had, good and bad, had prepared me for this very move. I resigned from teaching, sought license to preach by correspondence, entered the Course of Study School at Wesley Theological Seminary, and led the people of Galilee in a building program. It was pure joy! Especially the opportunity to preach regularly at the church and on invitation elsewhere. My determination to pursue a master of divinity degree delayed my ordination plans but equipped me with an understanding of the Scripture and the skill to synthesize new learnings with traditional and cultural experiences.

A former student of mine met me at the hospital where he is now an administrator and said to me, "Mrs. Kelly, somebody told me that you are teaching in the pulpit instead of preaching in the classroom!" Perhaps that was the transition. Anyway, I *am* black, woman, preacher. The six years at Galilee church enabled us to build and pay for a new church and to build a new parsonage. Preaching in the traditional style was a natural for that church and for me. I had established a relationship with the congregation as their former pastor's wife, and I had none of the hassle of trying to prove my calling. They shared it; indeed, they prompted it.

In 1972 Charles V. Hamilton's *The Black Preacher in America* appeared, the first full-length work ever published on the black preacher. Hamilton discusses historical, political, and cultural aspects of the black minister with particular emphasis on *his* many roles in the black church and in the black communities. This provocative study is authentic in its presentation and its conceptual exclusivity—the traditional black preacher is male. I read the book during my seminary days aware of the fact that, though black women ministers did exist in some denominations and women held positions of authority in apostolic circles, a definitive study as recent as 1972 felt no need to include them in a look at black ministry.

The black woman preacher does battle sexism, but she draws upon the spiritual confidence traditional in her culture. She is theologically and experientially grounded in a God who is Creator and Sustainer of the universe, actively holding the "whole world in his/her hands." She draws her understanding of a father/mother God from the traditional expression of the spiritual of her people, "He's my father, he's my mother, my sister and my brother, he's everything to me." The good news of the gospel of Jesus Christ is liberating from every societal binding. There is no way for a black woman to have understood the Christian witness of her people, who received the message of salvation from the very persons who enslaved them, without affirming her personhood sexually as well as racially.

The black woman preacher draws her strength from the strong sisterhood of the black church, which has historically supported the church and its educational institutions by cooking dinners, sponsoring programs, teaching Sunday school, training sons and daughters in Christian homes, encouraging black males to be the leaders in the church that society denied outside of it.

In leadership through women's groups black women developed skills of communication, but it was in the informality of the mid-week prayer service that they shared their daily experiences, hardships, and trials. It was here that one recognized the same rhythmic, tonal quality of the preacher. The pew became the pulpit, and the acts of God on behalf of his children were freely told by women in common and biblical wording. Sometimes the women were illiterate, but they were wise and their witness was sure. The spontaneous response gave assurance of understanding and knowing. Only men preached from the pulpit, but black male preachers acknowledge strong black church women who led them to Christ. A typical, traditional prayer meeting could be the setting for female "preaching." It would go something like this:

WOMAN: I *know* how Daniel felt in the Lion's Den!
RESPONSE: [Men, other women, and children] Yes!
WOMAN: I *know* how the Hebrew children felt in the
fiery furnace!
RESPONSE: [crescendos] YES!
[The "I knows" would continue in an ascending tonal
excitement with companion response until a cli-
mactic affirmation was spoken.]
WOMAN: But, like Job, I *know* that my Redeemer lives!
I *know* that he goes to prepare a place for me!
I *know* that this old world is not my home!

In the midst of the emotion-packed affirmation some personal experience of the week would be shared, and the testimony would come to a close on a peaceful plea:

WOMAN: Brothers and sisters, just pray for me that I
may *press* on! That I don't grow no ways weary [the
ascending tone begins again, and the entire group
is lifted with it], no ways tired. I just want to press
on to see what the end will be!

The "Amens" and "Thank you, Jesus" betrayed not only
the emotion of the moment, but the experiential sharing of a
common harshness of life. The emotional response testified
to faith in a God who would, in the end, bring victory to the
believer.

The unordained black woman has long been preacher-
spiritual leader. When you read the words of a Sojourner
Truth, you sense her style as traditional preaching. Harriet
Tubman moved on her faith and "preached" freedom on the
journey. Dr. Mary McCleod Bethune, founder and president
of Bethune-Cookman College, exhorted black women to
"stop playing bridge and start building bridges." Mrs. Nan-
nie Burroughs, Baptist woman educator, "preached" women
into early morning prayer meetings in Washington, D.C.,
years ago. I remember hearing the feet of many women who
responded to her powerful messages by walking to the early
morning prayer meetings in protest of the treatment of
blacks and women in the capital of our country. We were

told to stay in bed until our own mother returned from the meetings.

Barbara Jordan and Shirley Chisholm, both of whom served in Congress until recently, still attest in their speaking to the enthusiastic preaching style of many black pastors. The institution of Women's Day in the black church of practically all denominations gave opportunity for the development of "women speakers," who always began with the demure excuse, "Now, I'm really no preacher, but. . . ." Then they would proceed to preach the Word, really preach the Word in the completely identifiable black style, receiving the same response—even from the men. As long as it was a Women's Day celebration, this expression was acceptable.

Traditional black preaching, male or female, speaks out of this witnessing setting, gives it more formal exegisis, but continues its message of hope. It cannot be separated from the daily experiences of its listeners. The social dimension is clear: God is a God of love and justice. Jesus is the liberating Word of God. The preaching then relates itself to social and political issues. That which is "too controversial" for white pulpits is imperative for the black church. "Is there any word from the Lord?" is a query specific to the hope of the people.

Black churches, therefore, encourage their pastors to be active participants in community efforts to change conditions. Many of them seek public office as an extension of their ministry and preaching. It is difficult to preach the promise of abundant life without being actively engaged with those forces commensurate with the ideal. The congregation will follow their preacher beyond the sanctuary, and black churches are open to political and civic meetings marked by the same characteristics as black worship—good gospel singing, speaking in a preaching style, with audience response.

It is not difficult to see the simple transition from church leadership to the social movement of Dr. Martin Luther King and the present head of the Southern Christian Leadership Conference, Dr. Joseph Lowery, pastor of Central United Methodist Church, Atlanta. The powerful black preacher recognizes no cleavage between the purpose of the Spirit and the empowerment of a people. Witness today's Andrew Young, Jesse Jackson, and Benjamin Hooks. My preacher father was a member of the Ohio legislature, helping to write the civil rights laws of that state. I am one of three black ministers on the seven-member school board in Richmond, Virginia.

Black church bulletins on Sunday mornings often include information distributed by the National Association for the Advancement of Colored People and the Urban League, traditionally looked upon as extensions of the church in the community and often involving the same leadership. Present-day sermons deal with problems of unemployment, housing, health, education, and other root causes of crime and empty lives.

In the recent black awareness movement, the generation of black youth active in the '60s searched for their historical roots and found the black church in a firm position. It is the only network within the black community. Many, who had in harsh criticism left the church for peripheral social ministries, recognize the need for the black church to be once again the political, social, educational structure it was historically. They are returning, seeking a deeper faith, and it is significant that the new vocal response in worship consists of young voices. The same old phrases are used, and a generation of adults who have been "educated" to believe their traditional worship was a display of ignorance have recaptured the spirit of their grandparents and parents through the cultural acceptance of their children. Now when the word "Preach!" comes from the congregation, it may well be a young adult who wears blackness as a badge of honor and expresses the need to "feel something" once again.

With the return of young adults with analytical and social skills, the preaching style can again inspire action exemplified in urban ministries, strong community outreach, and the centrality of the church within the community. Evangelism in terms of membership growth may result from this stance, but it is not the major emphasis.

Witness an eight-year-old boy of our church community who is enrolled in our Church Hill Urban Ministry program (nicknamed CHUM). A strong component of the program is the children's section. On a certain evening he burst open the doors of the sanctuary during prayer meeting and loudly asked the question, "What's going on in *my* church?" The question was an evaluative one. He and his family are not members of Asbury Church; yet, in a very real sense, he called us to understand the responsibility of the church to the neighborhood and held us accountable for the very physical space we took up. We are indeed *his* church, and he has a right to demand an answer. Preaching in Asbury Church must speak to the needs of such a boy, who may never contribute a penny to the budget of the church. He is clearly what the good news is about.

The black woman preacher inherits the authenticity of the black church and its preaching. She seeks to preserve the warmth, the uninhibited response, the informality, the freedom of the tradition. It not only affirms her own self-concept but enables her to speak with compassion and biblical soundness to people of all colors, races, ages, and classes. Christianity, as it was intended, is a natural habitat for her faith. Christianity, as it is limited by cultural distinction, is the object of her confronting spirit. She preaches the Word of hope that sisters of all races will bind themselves together to model the reality that, "There is neither Jew nor Greek, there is neither slave nor free, there is neither male nor female; for all are one in Christ Jesus" (Gal. 3:28).

WOMEN
AND
LITURGY

Patricia Park

It was Reformation Sunday, 1974. The scene was the massive Gothic sanctuary of Riverside Church in New York City. Marshals kept watch as the church began to fill. There had been bomb threats, but in some ways the real "dynamite" was what was taking place in the last mainline Protestant denomination to approve the ordination of women. In July of that year eleven Episcopal women had been "irregularly" ordained in Philadelphia. Now, three months later, three of them were about to celebrate the Eucharist in public for the first time. They had been asked to wait until the validity of their ordinations had been resolved, but increasingly it was

The Rev. Patricia Park has served two Episcopal churches in Virginia, most recently as assistant rector of St. Paul's Episcopal Church in Richmond. Prior to that she was assistant to the rector of Immanuel Church-on-the-Hill in Alexandria. Ms. Park is a graduate of Madison College and Virginia Theological Seminary. She was co-chairperson of the National Coalition for the Ordination of Women to the Priesthood and Episcopacy and is currently president of the Episcopal Women's Caucus.

clear that would mean at least another two years. They could wait no longer. It was an electric moment in church history.

I was a deacon at the time. I had just finished seminary and was assistant to the rector at Immanuel Church-on-the-Hill in Alexandria, Virginia. I had been invited to participate in the service, and I well remember carrying my eight-month-old daughter in a pack on my back as we took the train from Washington to New York. When we arrived at Riverside, the air of excitement and anticipation was akin to what it had been in Philadelphia, where I had read the Gospel during the ordination service. Never before had I felt so powerful and spirit-filled by the energy of people in a liturgy. Never before had I had a clearer vision of the necessity for women priests and the power of women to serve God in their own image. Now we were to celebrate the service barred for centuries to women clergy in the Catholic tradition.

Bright yellow chasubles and dalmatics with orange crosses had been made for the priests and deacons taking part in the service. In the vesting room there was great tension; the press was everywhere. But when I put on my dalmatic I felt vested. It was so astonishingly bold and yet so necessary that women stand at the communion table. Sometimes I've experienced feelings of unworthiness from never having seen myself represented by another woman at the altar of God. But that day I was not afraid of being unworthy because I knew so well the grace and power of my sisters. Finally the procession lined up, and at the end—the place of honor—were the women. It seemed incredible.

A black gospel choir lead the procession, and women from other denominations were there to participate. But I was impatient. The first part of the service seemed to go on and on. I was familiar with women in the ministry of the Word. I yearned to see another woman bless and feed us with the body and blood of our Lord Jesus Christ. Finally the time came. Because I was the assisting deacon, I stood to Carter Heyward's right. She raised up her arms and sang, "The Lord be with you." The response came back, "And also with you."

"Lift up your hearts." "We lift them up unto the Lord." I was transfixed on that spot. The church seemed to radiate, and yet everything was curiously familiar. After communion people spoke and hugged and cried with each other. It was for me a powerful and positive experience of what Mary Daly calls "living on the boundary."

Why the power, the passion, and the pain? I believe it centers on the symbolic meanings that occur in liturgy, most specifically the liturgy of our Lord's Supper. As twentieth-century people, we often find it difficult to understand how deep religious symbols are in our unconscious as well as our conscious minds. To primitive and uneducated people the mysteries of life and death and God merge and flow together. Indians used to drink the blood of the deer so that they could run as fast as the deer and become like one. We eat the body and blood of Jesus, taking him into ourselves. We believe that God was a human being in the name and person of Jesus Christ, and we celebrate that love of God in a meal.

The word *liturgy* comes from two Greek words, *laos* (people) and *ergos* (work). Liturgy is, literally, the work of the people. In the Judeo-Christian tradition liturgy is a thoroughly social activity. The central feature of God's redemptive work is the covenant. Through the covenant with God Israel became a holy people; and through the new covenant in Jesus the church was called into being. Individuals come within the sphere of redemption through membership in the covenanted community. The nature of salvation is essentially social.[1]

In contemporary American culture perhaps the closest parallel we have is Thanksgiving. Thanksgiving is a national liturgy. It happens on a certain day. The people gather in specific groups, usually families. There is a certain menu, and each family and group has its own ritual for the day. Thanksgiving is an American cultic liturgy.

Our daily lives as well are filled with liturgies. Residents of many neighborhoods can almost set their watches by the early morning joggers or people walking their dogs. Another example is the liturgy in dating; it changes a little for each generation, but certain stages have to be passed in order to move into a relationship. Liturgies help us do what we don't know how else to do. They teach us. They comfort us. They speak a verbal and nonverbal language about who we are and what we value. Conversely, they also help us hide from God and each other. They are hard to change because again we are asked in our most comfortable and personal ways to live on the boundary, the unknown.

In the church's liturgy many details come into consideration. The priest has great power to set the tone and meaning of the event. Indeed, the priest at the altar is Christ's representative. It is here that the issue of women as leaders of the people of God and symbolic representatives of the church comes into focus. In the long debate which preceded the approval of the ordination of women in the Episcopal Church, a central issue was the maleness of Christ. Camps split over whether the emphasis should be on the particularity of the priest's sex or the priest as a *vehicle* of the reconciling act of Christ.[2]

But the issue is not solely one of theology or doctrine or tradition, as I tried to explain to a group of women seminarians recently. From their Protestant and highly intellectual vantage point they had great difficulty understanding why they have such a hard time being accepted by congregations. What is so threatening about their being pastors? What they did not understand was that women seeking to publicly represent the church are asking for a formal theological endorsement of the sexuality of women. In a woman's body somehow the issues of sex and religion merge. Women in religious leadership challenge the latent body-spirit dualism within Christianity. Images of women may be used to sell liquor, cars, and cigars, but not Jesus.

In an article which offers one of the most telling analyses of this phenomenon, Oberlin College psychologist John R. Thompson rehearses the ancient connection between evil and sexuality. He quotes from Hindu and Buddhist writings, as well as Islamic texts. In Christianity, he points out, the antiwoman bias had gained such momentum by the sixth century that the church actually took a vote on whether women were human beings.[3] The Christian fathers let women come to church provided they entered by the side door and kept their heads covered. Later women had to wear gloves, too, so as not to touch the church furnishings. And under no circumstances were women to receive the Eucharist into naked hands. Women were not allowed near the altar during mass or in the choir loft. Lest you are tempted to write this off as sixth-century mentality, says Thompson, remember that the last dictum against women in the choir loft was issued by the Vatican in 1971. "All too clearly, from the distant past to this very day comes the message that women are dangerous, evil temptresses, devious, tricky, needing to be watched."[4]

An anonymous writer gives this point of view contemporary application in terms of the priesthood: "How would you react to the presence of a pregnant woman in the pulpit? Giving absolution? How would you, the reader—male or female—react to the sight of a beautiful long-haired woman celebrating the Eucharist? Attractive yes, but also distracting."[5]

The writer was not asking idle questions. When I first went to my present parish, the gold earrings I wore became a source of controversy. The size of the earrings seemed to grow with each complaint. In a meeting with my rector, who was being put to a lot of grief over the issue, I was told to take them off. I protested that they were a symbol to me of my womanhood. Finally, however, I took them off, appearing in smaller ones three weeks later. Soon the issue died down.

It is one thing to understand all this intellectually; it is quite another thing to try to function as a professional woman knowing that others are carrying such preconceptions to their relationships with you. In the end it comes across as rejection, and it gets expressed in many ways. One of my worst experiences came shortly after I was ordained. An old man in the parish died while the rector was on vacation. When I went to call on the family, they made it unmistakably clear to me that I could do all the arrangements, counseling, and support of the family, but I could not be the liturgist at the funeral. Later I came to know the family and participated in the funeral of another member of the family, but the early rejection was so clearly based on my sex that it has stayed

with me. After six years in the parish ministry I have decided that it is part of my ministry, indeed integral to my call
by God, to be visible and present whether people are comfortable or not. The only way feelings about women will
change is that over the course of time the visibility of wom-
en clergy will change the symbols.

The outgrowth of my experiences of rejection most difficult for me to deal with has been the erosion of my feelings
of authority. Traditional authority has been passed down in
Catholic tradition through apostolic succession. I could almost see it passing to my male classmates in seminary. They
would begin to speak differently, or more firmly somehow.
They felt comfortable going out and buying clerical collars.
Their lives were beginning to take shape around their imitation of the men who taught them. They were modeling
themselves after their parish priests or other clergymen they
admired. Ecclesiastical authority begins with imitation and
then, I believe, moves into the theological—experiencing
one's personal call by God and seeing the verification of that
call by a Christian community. Since the Episcopal Church
was so ambivalent about ordaining women, the seminary so
patriarchal—lovingly so, I must add—I found it difficult to
find my own source of authority in the institution. Over the
years it has come from the lay people of the church and their
affirmation of my ministry, and it has come from my own
faith.

Authority is necessary in the institutional church. In liturgy of any kind, one must feel that he or she serves in a capacity of representation in order for the liturgy itself to have
authenticity. Recently a very old man in our parish died. I
did not know him well, but I knew his daughter, and I
helped the family plan the funeral. The interment was held
in an old cemetery in Richmond. The casket was to be placed
at the top of a hill. Behind me were two honorary pall bearers, both in their nineties, struggling up the hill. As I led
this procession, for one of the first times in my ordained life
I felt happy in a position of authority. I know it was because
I was wanted; I was able to be *the* representative person.

Death is a tense and stress-producing time no matter how
old the person who has died or the manner of death. Women

throughout time have buried their children in sickness and in childbirth and their men in wars. The liturgical function of women at the time of death, I believe, is and can be for many people a sign of hope. Their unconscious recognition of woman as the bearer of life may represent for people the ongoing nature of life. Because culturally it has been acceptable for women to cry and express emotion, their presence also may allow people to be more open about their grief. At the time of death we are radically confronted with the limitations of our humanity, our weakness and frailty.

I have often used the image of woman as the celebrant or president of the Holy Communion in this chapter because I believe that it is in this liturgy that the deepest meanings of Christianity are resident. It is at Holy Communion, the Lord's Supper, the Eucharist or mass—whatever word one uses to describe the blessing of bread and wine as the body and blood of our Lord Jesus Christ—that the Incarnation of God in Jesus and we the people as the body of Christ converge. This is the mystery of God which we call the Spirit acting in our lives. We come to the Lord's table as forgiven sinners, all of us. Woman as celebrant represents not only the unseen but the seen. She not only helps prepare the daily meals, she breaks the bread and serves the wine. She is not only nurturer, feeder of good foods, educator, and dishwasher, she also is worthy to be the representative of the people of God before God and God's most holy of tables and in the name of God's son. She is able to be both earthly and mysterious, authoritative and loving, intellectual and feeling, just as her brothers in Christ are able to be.

But there are other high liturgical moments in the church's life. It is necessary for women to be at the center of the entire sacramental life of the church from birth to death. At each of these liturgical functions we represent and symbolize to the body gathered the full humanity of life that Christ gave us.

Baptism is recognizing a new member of the body of Christ. Next to Holy Communion it is the chief focus of the liturgical life of the community. As a community, we bring the people into our midst, and they become part of us. We are responsible for each other. Most of my baptisms are of babies. A woman baptizing the baby, rather than being in the sentimentalized role of the one who gives birth as in the prevalent madonna and child image, is new for the church. Baptisms are one of the totally pure pleasures of my calling. Filled with beauty, joy, and celebration, they often have moments of humor in the uninhibited and unpredictable participation of the infants. Being a mother, I feel strongly that baptism during worship should be timed so both babies and parents can truly enjoy the service.

The role of the church in the performance of marriage is both legal and pastoral. I find premarital counseling a great opportunity for all kinds of theological reflection that the couple often have not shared with each other. The church's role at a wedding is to officiate; actually the couple marry each other. I believe my role is to make the marriage happen in a Christian atmosphere of both seriousness and joy. Being the officiant at a wedding is similar to giving a dinner party (another example of liturgy and ritual). The music, the candles, the processional all have to be considered and orchestrated. Liturgy is learning how to blend who we are—in this case the couple and their families—with the tradition of the church and the couple's own faith commitments.

One of the most precious parts of my priesthood is being able to give an absolution and blessing. It is an amazing and humbling experience to lift my hand over people and pronounce them absolved of their sins, in the name of Jesus Christ. The blessing that follows is the assurance again of God's continual love and comfort to the faithful. To stand before a congregation making the sign of the cross and saying the blessing of God gives me a feeling of being able to express the love of God through my arms and the sound of my voice and the look on my face. Truly at that point I represent the church to itself. It gives authority and hope to the people.

One writer has made the case for women with this observation:

Can a woman bless? It seems to me that the arms that have been extended in blessing over infant humanity

since the beginning of time might well be extended
in blessing over the bread and wine. . . . Can a woman
anoint? Have you ever thought that probably the first
oil that was ever put on you was put on you by a
woman? . . . Can a woman pronounce absolution? I
first learned the meaning of forgiveness and reconciliation from my mother, and it would be a familiar
and glad sound to my ear to hear the words of
priestly absolution said by a woman.[6]

In the Episcopal Church the liturgical functions of the
church are carefully spelled out in the *Book of Common Prayer*. My biggest problem with this book, as a liturgist, is that
of sexist language—for example, that in the Communion
service. Before the Peace is a passage called the Comfortable
Words: "This is a true saying, and worthy of all men to be received, that Christ Jesus came into the world to save sinners." Worthy of all *men*. Terrible and certainly not comfortable for me to say. In addition, I have a problem with God
the Creator *always* being father. Alas, I seem to remain a minority. Occasionally I change the words, and people often
don't notice or say anything; the subject does not affect
many people in the parish. In any event, I have chosen not
to fight my battle in the local parish on the issue of sexist
language because it blocks other forms of communication.
Along with others, however, I do intend to press systematically for changes in the liturgy.

The problem with masculine language is that it is in itself
a symbol of the woman who is not seen, known, or public.
She is never named by her sex, except negatively, though it
is assumed that *woman* is incorporated with the word *man*.
The true identity of woman is not known. She is defined in
terms of her relationship to man and his world. The dilemma this brings for women and liturgy is spelled out by Nelle
Morton:

Women appear at an impasse in celebration. Traditional symbols root too deeply in a patriarchal culture
to function adequately in their new context, and new
symbols have not yet emerged.

The search for symbols seems to take the form of a "no-saying" and a "yes-saying" in which we see both the no and the yes as positive. We are not saying no to the whole created order of things—our traditions and ourselves included—we are saying no to those images, symbols, structures, and practices which cripple us and keep us from claiming our rightful personhood. We are saying no to a system that legitimates these images through cosmic myths, language, and daily dramas of etiquette.

We began our "no" by substituting feminine words of liturgy for those masculine words that exclude women. But soon we found that word change was not enough. The masculine words had conjured up images that continued to persist in the community psyche to proclaim gender instead of humanness. But the change provided affirmation of ourselves as persons and enabled us to hear that life is for us— directly, wholly, and lovingly.[7]

The sacraments of the church are public markings of all that we do in our daily lives. They are where holy and everyday come together and have meaning and witness. The freedom of men and women to use their gifts hardly has been tapped. We know that in the death of the patriarchy we are in a wilderness, and often we are lonely and afraid. We do not know how long we will be there. But it is an exciting time, too. We survive knowing that we have the gift of the Holy Spirit of God with us. We are not abandoned. I know that *I* grow less afraid every day.

Notes

1. Charles L. Winters, Jr., *Education for Ministry*, Part Two, Book Two (Sewanee, Tenn.: University of the South, School of Theology, 1975), p. 228.

2. For a brief summary of the issue see Rosemary Ruether and Eleanor McLaughlin, eds., *Women of Spirit: Female Leadership in the Jewish and Christian Traditions* (New

York: Simon and Schuster, 1979), pp. 366–70.

3. John R. Thompson, "Psychic Sources of Misogyny," *Christianity and Crisis*, April 2, 1979, p. 75.

4. Ibid.

5. Cited in Michael P. Hamilton and Nancy S. Montgomery, eds., *The Ordination of Women: Pro and Con* (New

York: Morehouse-Barlow, 1975), p. 48.

6. Frederick A. Fenton, "Can a Woman . . . ?" *Christianity and Crisis*, July 23, 1973, p. 150.

7. Carol P. Christ and Judith Plaskow, eds., *Womanspirit Rising: A Feminist Reader in Religion* (San Francisco: Harper & Row, 1979), p. 159.

A MINISTRY OF PRESENCE

Brita Gill

It is 4:45, and I am preparing to leave the office for a rare early night home. The phone rings, and a young woman's voice on the other end says, "I need help and would like to see a minister." I ask her if she can briefly tell me what is troubling her. She says, "No, I can't talk here."

"Could you come in tomorrow?"

"Oh, no. Please, won't you see me today? I don't know if I can go through one more day. I must see you today."

"OK. Can you come now?"

"No, I work until six."

"All right, come right after work."

An hour and a half later an exhausted, hassled, exasperated young woman of twenty-six is sitting on my office couch. I am the first person, she says, who hasn't tried to refer her

The Rev. Brita Gill is pastor of First Congregational Church in Alameda, California. She was associate minister of First Congregational Church in San Francisco when she wrote this chapter. Ms. Gill is a graduate of the University of California at Berkeley and Harvard Divinity School. She is enrolled in doctoral studies in personality sciences and religion at the Graduate Theological Union in Berkeley.

somewhere else. She is newly arrived in the city with her seven-year-old daughter, having just left "a bad scene" with her husband in the East. She is earning three dollars an hour at a local department store and trying to support herself and her child. She is sick and obviously in generally poor health. She is barely making it, but she is. It is just hard and lonely.

She talks and talks, with tears at the beginning and end as she unfolds all that has brought her to this moment. She asks if she may leave some luggage in my office. She was assaulted in the lobby of her apartment building and moved out without having found another place to live.

This visit was the beginning of several meetings and telephone calls dealing not only with the emotional turmoil of her life but with the nitty-gritty of making it in the city— poor, single, and with a child. For several days her belongings sat in my office reminding me of her burden, the heaviness of her life and all that she could not leave behind.

In the weeks that followed, as I tried to help this woman, I once again learned the gift and limitations of being a pastor in the city. The gift was being able to care and to help someone in whatever way I could. The limitations were many: housing shortages, unjust wages, discrimination against children in apartment rentals, and the fact that she was one of many who would need my time and attention that week. Such pastoral concerns lead me to the larger struggles against injustices in the city. But these activities also take time from the personal side of ministry. One of the hardest lessons has been accepting my limitations in helping others. I must continually remind myself that although I cannot do everything, I can do something.

This encounter, though in its own way unique, demanded what is again and again required of a clergywoman with major responsibilities in pastoral counseling in an urban church. It is what I call "a ministry of presence"—a ministry that is oriented to individuals, not just to problems. It is easy, when confronted with so much suffering on a daily basis in the city, to forget the face and to see only the problem. It is a self-protective way by which we minimize the impact of others on our lives and avoid what they may be asking of us.

Yet as a minister of the gospel of Jesus Christ, I must catch myself when this begins to happen. It is too easy to put individuals into categories—the hungry, the homeless, the psychotic, the drunk—and thereby discount them and my responsibility to them as unique persons. As a minister, I must remember that each person is totally distinct, and therefore his or her situation is unique.

A ministry of presence through pastoral counseling is characterized not so much by the skill, knowledge, or technique of the pastor as by the minister's manner of being with another. It is a ministry of being, not merely of doing.

I cannot heal another person; I can only create the environment and relationship where God's healing may take place. I must let go of the incessantly busy Martha within me and let her sister Mary be hostess. (Mary offers hospitality to the stranger not by "doing for" but by creating the kind of space in which the stranger is made to feel welcome and by being receptive to what this person brings.) My first act of engagement with another person should be one not of self-assertion, but of making a space where the other feels his or her presence is received.

What I am asked to be and to do is made easier, in part, by the fact that, like many women, I was raised to be relationally oriented. Women in our society have survived by being exceptionally sensitive to the unstated and subtle aspects of relationship. In many cases women have developed as second nature an ear that is geared to attentive listening.

It is in being a good listener that one is the most enabling counselor. However, it is not a passive listening in which I withdraw from any emotional involvement, not a listening that is simply a vehicle for a person to dump whatever is on his or her heart or mind. Rather, it is an involved listening that helps focus the communication. Ultimately, my listening helps the person hear him- or herself. It is a listening that requires me to step over to the other side to hear with the other's ears and see with his or her eyes. For me to listen means to be able to experience what that person is feeling. It means to put myself in the other context and to be open to the vulnerability that person is feeling. This is often frightening, for it requires me to open myself to so many cries of pain, loneliness, despair, stagnation, meaninglessness, and ambivalence. Yet there is not a ministry of presence without this kind of opening.

A ministry of presence incarnates self-giving love. It knows that the sacred is not something set apart but something that dwells in the concreteness of our daily existence. "As you do it unto the least of these, you do it unto me." In bringing our full presence to an encounter, we meet Christ and touch the eternal.

A legend from the Talmud illustrates how it is precisely in reaching out to our neighbor in self-giving love that we reach the eternal. A rabbi disappears from the synagogue for a few hours every Day of Atonement. One of his followers suspects that he is secretly meeting the Almighty and follows him. He watches as the rabbi puts on coarse peasant clothes and cares for an invalid woman in a cottage, cleaning out her room and preparing food for her. The follower goes back to the synagogue. And when he is asked, "Did the rabbi ascend to heaven?" he replies, "If not higher."

The eternal is not something one attains in the beyond; it is the transcendent dimension that is immanent in what Martin Buber calls "real meeting." Buber observes, "God is present when I confront you, but if I look away from you, I ignore him. As long as I merely experience or use you I deny God, but when I encounter you, I encounter Him."[1]

A ministry of presence allows the sacred to unfold in each of us and between us. A ministry of presence reminds us that God's revelation does not come to us in the discovery of specific knowledge about God's essence as much as it does in the unfolding of an ever-faithful Presence. In our being faithful to one another in the encounters of our lives, we are reminded of God's faithfulness to us.

Yet, life is such that we are moved and touched by more people, relationships, and events than we have the time or energy to be responsive to. We must make the difficult choices that our finitude necessitates. Out of those choices emerge an overwhelming number of questions and concerns for theological reflection. It is precisely at those times when we feel most vulnerable, anxious, and in crisis—when our world and lives have been jolted in some major way—that faith and our own experience must be in dialogue. In pastoral counseling this is an ongoing process.

In a single week of ministry in the city I am asked to be responsive to countless individuals and to the concerns and questions their presence raises. In one such week I am awakened at 6:15 by a phone call from a mental patient at a local hospital who wants me to be her legal guardian to oversee her Social Security checks. I have never met this woman, but she heard me preach once and thinks I would be a person who cares. What do I owe this person? To say yes here means to say no elsewhere. Do I have the energy to make such a commitment? Are there other options that don't include me?

Three people die: a lonely, abandoned church member dies in a home removed from the city; a middle-aged woman dies of cancer; a former counselee is assaulted and murdered, her naked body found on a street three blocks from the church. In the midst of death, so many questions. Did it have to end this way? What does a dying woman need most? What genuinely comforts those who grieve?

A man whose marriage ceremony I performed drops in to tell me that his son is gay. He is ashamed, bewildered, groping. I am the first one besides his wife with whom he has discussed this. What will enable this man to love and accept his son? Will he learn to accept himself as a father of a gay son? What is it that really bothers him about his son's being gay?

I make four visits to four different hospitals and see a seventy-six-year-old woman recovering from heart surgery, a man dying of cancer, a woman who has just been told that her only child has two months to live, and the new mother of a nine-pound, thirteen-ounce baby boy. Sickness and health, death and birth, joy and sorrow—these are all part of God's creation. How do we claim the wholeness of life without seeking only to hold on to a part? How do we respond to unanswerable questions like that of the mother who asked, "Why my daughter and not me?"

That same week there are appointments for marriage

counseling with six people whose lives are shaky and uncertain. They are questioning the commitment they once made. Feelings of loneliness, hopelessness, fear, and desperation arise in these painful encounters. There are profound feelings of loss and sadness. Where is there hope for these individuals or for their marriages? What would wholeness mean for them? Does human finitude make some distances too great to bridge?

There is counseling with a young woman who is bored with life and her work. She is so isolated that her only conversational contact outside her work is our regularly scheduled hour. What has locked this person inside herself? What does, or could, the church mean for her?

Seven walk-ins off the street ask for money for food, shelter, and transportation. How much time will I give to each of these people? Why will I say yes to one and no to another? If I say no, have I sensed his or her real need and tried to address it? Can I forgive myself when my strength is spent and I'm too tired to really care?

I walk down Powell Street for a lunch appointment and see a paraplegic, a young man playing a guitar with arms that have only stubs for hands, a beggar with a harmonica and a tin cup, a man without legs on a skateboard, a very young prostitute covered with makeup, a screaming man whose experience is imperceptible to people around him. The despair of the city takes hold of me. How do I let the suffering in without letting it overwhelm me or harden my heart against it? How do I, will I, respond to these and others?

Our lives are never more profoundly touched or inalterably changed than at the place of suffering. It is an experience we cannot escape. Yet often we attempt to turn our eyes away from rather than toward other people's suffering.

Women, perhaps because of biological necessity, have come to accept pain more easily than men. Childbirth teaches us that we must go with the pain and not resist it. If we resist, we cut off the life that is trying to be born. We must help people do the same thing with spiritual pain. Helping people hear and listen to the inner cry is often the beginning of their spiritual journey. We do not aid them by helping them flee from their pain, but by offering a presence that allows them to listen to their pain so that something new may be born. Not only is our more ready acceptance of pain a part of our identity as women, it is integral to our identity as followers of Christ.

From the cross Jesus turns to his mother and beloved disciple and says: "Woman, behold your son!" And to the beloved disciple he says, "Behold your mother!" Jesus does not tell them or us to go away from the cross but to "behold." Behold the one sitting, standing, living in your midst. To behold the feelings, the condition, and circumstances of another is to transcend the boundaries of the self and to take in the reality of another.

In an interview for the British Broadcasting Company, a woman who was dying of cancer made an astonishing observation about Jesus and his mother at the cross. The interviewer, a clergyman, confessed that when he is faced with his own death he would like to go away to some secret place so his wife and children will be spared the heartache of seeing him "go a bit peculiar in the head or go in coma, and all this sort of stuff." The woman, from the depth of her pain yet sustained by her faith, made this reply: "Our Lord carried his cross to Calvary and his mother followed him. And she was the sort of mother who would stand at the foot of the cross when her son was crucified. And he was the sort of son who would let her. And what more perfect love, and what more perfect understanding could there be than that? Can't you let us do the same? Can't we love each other in that way—in him?"[2]

Mary and the beloved disciple stand in the shadow of the cross, dazed, bewildered, stunned, enduring the agony of the one they love. Jesus, knowing that their eyes are transfixed on him and his suffering, transforms their pain in a new awareness.

"Behold!" The imperative he gives us is to see, to gaze upon, to hold in one's sight, to keep one's attention on the other. In speaking he summons the mourners to call forth the relational resources in their midst. The beloved disciple and Mary now see not simply the agony of the crucified one but the sorrow of each other. What they cannot do for Jesus, nor Jesus for them, they can do for one another.

It is never our task as pastors to assure others that all will be well. Rather, it is to give them the confidence that we will be with them and stand by them in the midst of their struggles and uncertainties. Our task as clergywomen is not to turn our eyes away from suffering but to help people find ways to move through it, transforming it into new awareness and new possibility. It is in faithful presence, our standing with them, that they may first find the courage to face what is so they can feel empowered to move to what might be.

A person is born into community. Human existence is designed to be lived, at least in part, with and for people. There is no such thing as a self alone, only a self in the world. Paul Tillich in *The Courage to Be* speaks of how the identity of participation is an identity in the power of being. It is not merely a matter of having the courage to be as oneself but the courage to be a participant. "Only in the continuous encounter with other persons does the person become and remain a person. The place of this encounter is community."[3]

A person in counseling may begin on the fringes of community, but that person must be regarded as a communal, and not just a solitary, being. As pastoral counselors, we need to foster those aspects of the person which are actualized within community or in relations with others. We most often help people deal with questions of relationships in their lives, so we must aid them not only in the inner struggle but in their external life as well.

Women today have found new strength and hope in their solidarity with other women and in the communal nature of their struggle. They know the healing effect of community. This consciousness is a gift that can be lifted up in an important way in the context of pastoral counseling and care in a church.

Women, who have a primary identity as relational selves, are in a place to draw upon the community as one resource in healing. Classes, small groups, social gatherings, and meetings all can be occasions for healing. The healing resources that lie within a church provide the pastoral counselor with a unique asset.

One very isolated and fearful woman who was in counseling with me began to attend church and participate in some of its functions. She said to me, "This is the only place I have experienced such unreserved acceptance." A man with real talents but very isolated came to find meaningful relationships and a sense of purpose as a member of one of the church boards. Another man, who was going through a divorce, was able to find a community where his new identity as a single male could be accepted and where new friends could be found. In a downtown church, where loneliness is one of people's predominant concerns, there is no substitute for the healing that comes from a sense of belonging. The church is a place where people minister to one another. The Holy Spirit and the gracious healing of God may happen "in the between" anywhere in the life of the church.

A ministry of presence requires a patient waiting, an attentive attitude, and total receptivity. We have to know that the soul seeking wholeness has its own time, its own period of gestation. Just as nine months of pregnancy cannot be rushed, neither can the time it takes a human being to grow or heal. Our counseling must be done prayerfully, allowing and trusting that God's healing presence will be there. As we let go of our need to cure, God may use our caring.

Trying to assess the unique gifts women bring to the role of pastoral counselor is not easy, because generalizations always cloud the larger truth. In this case it is made more difficult by the fact that many men who are attracted to ministry have developed or possess qualities that often are labeled as gifts of the feminine.

Initially, congregations may be reluctant to accept women in the pulpit, but I have found that individual members find few difficulties in going to a woman for pastoral counseling. Perhaps this is because traditionally authority has been more readily bestowed on women in the private spheres of life than in the public arenas. Only recently has this situation begun to change significantly. (Ultimately, our authority as women or men in ministry has its source in our vocation as servants of Jesus Christ. It is God who grants us authority when we are open to such leading. As Daniel Day Williams observed, "The crisis of authority is the crisis of faith itself."[4] We must trust continually that what we are able to do and be comes only through our receptivity to God's leading.)

A part of every clergywoman's journey, I would venture to say, has included much self-reflection and self-assessment. Too many questions have been raised along the way for such women not to have done some in-depth self-examination. Any good counselor needs to have a high sense of self-awareness and to have undertaken the same intensity of self-exploration that she asks of others. The effects of the women's movement have been such that women struggle with their past, present, and future in an intense and whole-hearted way, privately, in therapy, and in groups. Questions of identity, self-confidence, meaninglessness, purposefulness, work relationships, loss, despair, and religious concerns have all catapulted women from a lack of self-awareness to an incredible new self-consciousness. This experience has been and is a rich asset to women involved in pastoral counseling. They know that they share in the same struggles and predicaments as others. This is not intellectual acknowledgement; it is the assent of experience.

Because most women have been raised to be relationally oriented, they have, perhaps, less need or desire to give into what I call "the professionalization of relationship." Frequently people find their place of greatest intimacy in a weekly appointment with a psychiatrist or psychologist. I do not deny the need for these professionals, but too often too much of too many lives is relegated to the isolation of an office. As a result, our most intimate relationships have become professionalized. The parish, by its very nature, has a built-in resistance to the professionalization of relationship. More often than not a relationship between a minister and a parishioner exists before a counseling situation. Trust has often been established beforehand, a trust tied to the kind of person one is as a minister.

I am not known to my counselees simply as a counselor or therapist, nor they to me simply as counselees. Belonging to the same church community makes our relationship multi-faceted. In one week we may worship together, work on the same committee, socialize at a party, and mourn the loss of a common friend. I am likely to know the significant people in their lives. Trust is enabled when people sense that you know them as a whole people. You see them not only at their pained places of existence, but in many settings and in many interactions.

It is also the case within the Christian community that if a relationship lacks reciprocity, it appears artificial. This does not mean it is necessary or even wise in a counseling situation to share frequently from my own life experience, but it does mean that I am open and sensitive to what is most fitting and growth-producing for the counselee. There is a desire to eliminate boundaries between theory and life.

Clergywomen may have an advantage in one important respect: Often we are the first woman minister a person has met, so we may carry fewer stereotypes with us. Frequent comments are: "You sure aren't like all the ministers I have known"; "You don't look like a minister"; "You're a different kind of minister." Freedom from stereotyped images tends to elicit responses that people might be more reluctant to share elsewhere, and gives us the opportunity to shape the encounter as we see necessary. On the other hand, others may be inhibited until trust is built.

For many women a woman in a nontraditional woman's role as a counselor is a helpful and encouraging model. Through you they begin to dialogue with unacknowledged or newly awakened parts of themselves. As a clergywoman, I often think of myself in the role of midwife, one who does not create something new but stands patiently by, helping the other give birth to newfound parts of her- or himself.

By their very presence in ministry, women open up questions of vulnerability for those in the congregation. The unexpected, unanticipated opens up queries not previously addressed with the same intensity. Seeing women in a role that has traditionally been viewed as male raises questions about many assumptions, attitudes, and presuppositions upon which people have built their lives and sometimes even their faith. Women's tendency to be more vulnerable than men also readily opens the places of hurt and sensitivity in other persons' lives. This is often scary, for with increased vulnerability comes the fear of a loss of control and image. Though it is frightening, our ability to be vulnerable with one another is essential to loving relationships. I am reminded of the Jewish story about the enthusiastic disciple who told his rabbi that he loved him. The rabbi asked, "Do you know what hurts me?" When the disciple said, "No," the rabbi replied, "If you do not know what hurts me, how can you say you love me?"

Several women have sought me out specifically because I am a woman. For many women the male pastor often has been an intimidating presence and one with whom they feel they have to protect their image. Some find more permission to be vulnerable with a woman. Struggles with sexuality and mothering are raised with less self-consciousness and without as much fear of loss of self-esteem. Could it be that clergywomen do not carry the stereotype of the judgmental pastor?

My identity as a feminist and my identity as a Christian clergywoman do not conflict; each creatively informs the other. Part of pastoral counseling is consciousness-raising: We need to help the counselee reflect on what is happening. Where am I? Where do I want to go? We need to be particularly careful that we are not simply helping the other person adjust to current cultural expectations. Our own experience has increased our sensitivity to how we all suffer unnecessarily. As Henri Nouwen has written, "One of our tasks as ministers is to help people from suffering for the wrong reasons."[5]

Being a woman also can be helpful in marriage counseling. Often it is the wife who insists on seeing a woman counselor, and the man comes along with the feeling that it is going to be "two against one." Many couples I have worked with are in very painful struggles of changing self-awareness and role expectation. Stagnation has caused the relationship to deteriorate to a function and role orientation ("I'll do this if you do that"), and couples seek a key to greater intimacy. Cataclysmic changes taking place in the woman's life often throw the relationship out of balance. Women's changing self-perceptions have had a powerful effect on relationships. Some women who married with the hope that they would be taken care of are now expressing a need to be seen as whole women, not as indulged children. As women grow stronger, with a greater sense of self, much of what has been taken for granted in relationship gets called into question.

On the whole, I find young men, more than young women, to be unsure of themselves. Men feel threatened in what they perceive as their masculine role because they frequently see women as rivals rather than partners. They have been raised to be competitive, but not with their wives and lovers. Young women, on the other hand, are standing in newfound places of recognition and status. They continue to be wives and mothers, yet they are successful in a "man's world" as well. Often they fail to see how uncertain and precarious men feel and how they need to be affirmed.

In the struggle for more depth, communication, understanding, and acceptance in the marriage relationship, men, I believe, find it very helpful to know that I am "for them." To know that I am able to see their side and to feel their loss and vulnerability decreases the sense of polarization and feeling of "over-againstness" at a critical time in their lives. Support from a woman who is for both partners in marriage offers hope.

It is important to state that clergywomen can be as important an influence in men's lives as in women's. I am a minister not simply for women; I care with the same intensity about the well-being of men. For many men it is less threatening to be vulnerable with a woman than with a man; they do not feel the need to protect an image they may need to project elsewhere. Often they find it easier to be in touch with their anger. In some respects it is easier for men to direct anger toward a woman; unfortunately, however, this is often because they feel more entitled. Women in positions of authority and responsibility will inevitably experience some projection of men's unworked-through attitudes and relationships with women.

Beyond the special possibilities open to clergywomen in pastoral counseling, however, there are also special temptations.

Women's upbringing has most often included the much-needed qualities of good counseling: nurturing, supportive, accepting, nonjudgmental ways of interacting. For many counselees there is an increased feeling of safeness simply because the counselor is a woman. This can undermine the enabling relationship if we are not aware of it.

The safety a counselee might initially feel with you because you are a woman can potentially undermine growth in the relationship. Although the initial building of rapport may be eased, the inherent hazard is the temptation to get stuck in compassion without being able to move to confrontation and objectivity. We must take our role and presence seriously ourselves as well as asking to be taken seriously.

We must not fall into the easy role of simply being a "hurtsoother." My office is not a place to dump hurt and negative feelings while I sit listening passively and finally apply a Band-Aid. I am there not simply to share in the pain but also to affirm the other as he or she struggles. My vocation as a Christian minister is not to treat my counselees as children but to assist them in the kind of growth that leads toward greater wholeness and responsibility.

I must avoid the temptation to be shaped into what they think they need from me. Women have succumbed to this temptation in many different ways, with detriment to themselves and others.

The church remains an easy target for projection and a paradigm for unresolved and conflicted parental relationships. It is also too easy, and at times self-satisfying, for the minister to play the surrogate parent. We must resist the temptation to play "supermother" by inappropriately taking on the role of parent for another person. That is not to say that the nurturing parent is not sometimes needed, but we must not let ourselves become a substitute for a relationship that needs to be reworked somewhere else. And we must never "parent" in such a way as to interfere with the growth of another. To allow ourselves to assume the parental role helps others to evade their responsibility.

A temptation women who are mothers know only too well is to want to hold on when it is time to let go. As the other person grows, so must I. I need to accept and even demonstrate the possibility of a change in relationship. There needs to be the sensitivity to know when it is time to withdraw. A model for this can be found in the Jewish mystical doctrine of *Tsimtsum*: "God as omnipresent and omnipotent was everywhere. God filled the universe with his being. How then could the creation come about? God had to create by withdrawal. God created the not Him, the other, by self-concentration. On the human level, withdrawal of myself aids the other to come into being."[6]

The letting go happens as we make space for the reality of another to unfold and as we become increasingly sensitive to the time when we are not needed. The pastor, because of her multifaceted relationships with the congregation, has the challenging opportunity to let the relationship take new form and shape. As the other matures, so must the nature of the relationship.

One temptation that I believe women are particularly prone to is over-accessibility. People feel less reluctance in calling upon a woman than a man when anything—major or minor—is on their mind. They also seem to feel little hesitation in raising the trivial and inconsequential. The sense people carry for women as the maternal presence, receptive and inviting, often leave us feeling used and abused, with minimum time for ourselves. Women traditionally have lived to satisfy the needs of others. If this is done at the expense of self-nurturing, the nurturing mother becomes depleted sooner or later.

Because people find it relatively easy and unthreatening to ask something of a woman, we must learn the necessity of sometimes saying no. Without a no there cannot be a genuine yes. Without the no, we lose all sense of boundaries, as well as the humility necessary to know that we cannot be all things to all people. Without learning to say no, and even at times making ourselves unavailable, we risk resenting others who ask for our time and attention. Experience continually teaches me that when we meet our own deepest needs, we are also more inclined to serve others' real needs.

Closely tied to this is the temptation of overgiving, well known as the mother's suffocating love. Giving without boundaries or discrimination can stifle or cripple others in development. It also leaves them feeling an unfair burden of indebtedness. Giving what is not needed chokes and kills and may lead to infantile behavior rather than maturity. To love another means to know the need and to give proportionately. Sometimes we overgive when we get caught in the trap of thinking that it is we who heal, rather than God. No matter how loving, understanding, or skillful we may be, God does not always work through us in the ways we might hope.

Finally, and understandably, there is the temptation to take on the male value system, structures, and ways of doing ministry by not trusting our own perceptions and experiences or following our intuitions. One issue men struggle with, and one which women are coming to terms with, is seeing ministry as primarily something we *do* rather than a manner of *being*—being in relationship to others in all we do. To get caught in overactivity, mental or physical, interferes with depth relationships with God and other people. When our work becomes primary, we have lost our calling as women and ministers of the gospel. Whenever women take on the role of minister and define their work by their function, loss of full human identity will occur. We must remember that our vocation has a face and a humanity; we must not think of ourselves as simply professionals performing a role. Although our identity is as workers, our task is relationship.

There is a need for women to model a kind of relationship that influences the whole quality of interactions within a parish. I am convinced that congregations are diminished by hierarchical structures. One goal of Christian feminists is to develop and work in less hierarchical structures. We murder people's relational capacity if the critical and depth relationships are seen as only between clergy and congregation, or if the clergy's primary concern is with vertical versus horizontal relationships. We need a relational perspective to influence the very church structures that often interfere or hinder relationships built on mutuality, reciprocity, and equality. We need to create structures within community that really allow for dialogue. We are programmed to death but have a blindness to relationship in too many areas of church life.

Ultimately, it is not any one function that will reveal our identity and our calling as clergywomen, but our capacity for strengthening loving and humanizing relationships. We must resist the temptation as clergywomen to be relegated to any one role or function. We must be seen in all arenas in the life of the congregation so that we and the congregation will have the opportunity to relate to one another on many levels, and so that we can facilitate a greater involvement and relatedness among the people in all facets of church life. Each arena of ministry—be it preaching, teaching, administration, pastoral counseling, or care—is a place where we can reach out to others with a ministry of presence and help them to do the same for one another. We must avoid the danger of limiting the relational perspective we embody to any one aspect of church life. This perspective needs to be lifted up and celebrated, modeled and affirmed, respected and followed in the most public as well as the most private spheres of ministry.

Notes

1. Martin Buber, *I and Thou* (New York: Charles Scribner's Sons, 1970), p. 28.

2. Charles McCoy and Marjorie Casebier McCoy, *The Transforming Cross* (Nashville: Abingdon Press, 1977), p. 53.

3. Paul Tillich, *The Courage to*

Be (New Haven, Conn.: Yale University Press, 1952), p. 91.

4. Daniel Day Williams, *The Minister and the Care of Souls* (New York: Harper & Row, 1961), p. 45.

5. Henri Nouwen, *The Wounded Healer* (Garden City, New York: Doubleday, 1979), p. 93.

6. James Hillman, *Insearch* (New York: Charles Scribner's Sons, 1967), p. 31.

BEARING
THE
GOOD
NEWS

Dianna Pohlman Bell

Two new pastors arrived just in time to begin the fall activities in the parish. Hopeful anticipation pulsed through congregation and pastors alike, for this was a new partnership in ministry for everyone. By Advent there was a sense of trust developing, and Lent found a real solidarity of relationship between the co-pastors as well as between the pastors and the congregation. The newness was giving way to a satisfying pace. Nevertheless, shortly after Easter another life began which was somewhat different from the new-life celebrations characteristic of either Christmas or Easter. One pastor developed a queasy sickness. It was a persistent, low-grade discomfort sufficient to dull her recently discovered

---

The Rev. Dianna Pohlman Bell is pastor of the United Presbyterian Church of La Mirada, California. Her husband serves as associate pastor. Ms. Bell is a graduate of Occidental College, with a degree in music, and Princeton Theological Seminary. She was the first woman to serve as a chaplain in the United States military.

joy in parish ministry. Time and tests proved the evident: pregnancy.

A month later, when the news became public, the congregation began a new kind of witness. "Our pastor is going to have a baby!" they exclaimed. A twenty-year-old, medium-sized congregation, children grown and leaving, grandchildren yet to appear, a sagging church school, a changing community unresponsive to a steady church presence—all the elements of a corporate mid-life crisis. Then, "We're going to have a baby!" They suddenly felt a new potency, a rediscovery that they were bearers of good news.

Good news is the message of the church. God is Creator, Redeemer, and Comforter, and this is good news for the world. Witnessing to this message is understood as evangelism. As a task of the church, evangelism has become increasingly influenced, in purpose and form, by the world outside rather than by the Spirit within. This chapter is an attempt to rethink the nature and meaning of evangelism, from a biblical perspective, through a woman's experience, toward an increasingly whole and faithful witness.

One who bears good news is called *evangel*. This Greek term has early Hebrew roots (*basar*) with a salient heritage. The evangel (*mebaser*) was a messenger sent from the scene of battle to carry the news of victory. Early secular usage gave way to increasing religious use as seen progressively through 1 Samuel 31:9; 1 Chronicles 10:9; 2 Samuel 1:20; 18:19–21; Psalms 68:11 and 40:10.[1]

The concept of the messenger of a battle victory seen in a strictly human sense, however, does not do full justice to the messenger/proclaimer role which characterizes the activity of God in the Old Testament. Deutero-Isaiah describes the *mebaser* as one who is seen leading the people as they return from their Babylonian captivity; those who await them in Zion strain with intense anticipation to hear of the victory:

How beautiful upon the mountains
  are the feet of [the one] who brings good tidings,
who publishes peace, who brings good tidings of good,

who publishes salvation,
who says to Zion, "Your God reigns."
[Isa. 52:7]

Evangel. The word becomes more than a simple term for a person who bears good news; it is God's self-witness. The theologian-writers of Scripture sensed that the whole activity of God was a message of victory. The creation story in the first chapter of Genesis focuses on victory: Light was made the victor over all-engulfing darkness; the firmament of heaven was established to separate the waters, thereby harnessing their power and terror, greatly feared by the ancient mind. For the further restraint of the waters, God gathered them together in one place allowing hospitable dry land to appear. Only after these most basic controls were established over the powers of death did God proceed to create life in its various forms.

The Exodus story also focuses on victory. A people who knew only bondage to a foreign power found themselves free at last. Fearful and discouraged, they were threatened with destruction from within. But they left that state of corporate death to enter (albeit, at times unwillingly) a wilderness of re-creation where God prepared them to enter a new land of their own. Moses lead them as God's evangel of victory.

The Babylonian exile, too, was an opportunity for God to proclaim victory. What would appear to the exiled Israelites as a hopeless condition is again transformed by God. The Servant of the Lord proclaims:

The Spirit of the Lord GOD is upon me,
　　because the LORD has anointed me
to bring good tidings to the afflicted;
　　he has sent me to bind up the brokenhearted,
to proclaim liberty to the captives,
　　and the opening of the prison to those who are bound;
to proclaim the year of the LORD's favor,
　　and the day of vengeance of our God;
to comfort all who mourn. . . .　　　　　[Isa. 61:1–2]

Consistently the Old Testament reveals a God who is sovereign, victorious over all which would threaten to harm or destroy. Everything God had been demonstrating throughout the history of Israel was then translated into flesh and blood in the person of Jesus the Christ. Jesus' whole life was as one sent from the scene of victorious battle.[2]

> But you, O Bethlehem Ephrathah,
>   who are little to be among the clans of Judah,
> from you shall come forth for me
>   one who is to be ruler of Israel,
> whose origin is from old, from ancient ways.
> [Mic. 5:2]

This ancient prophecy of kingly origins in an unassuming place was interpreted as Jesus' own origin (Matt. 2:6), an origin which even in retrospect was regarded as highly suspect as a source of any good news (John 7:40–43). A messenger of victory is here seen emerging not from the glorious field of battle but from a simple, ordinary village.

> A voice was heard in Ramah,
> wailing and loud lamentation,
> Rachel weeping for her children;
> she refused to be consoled,
> because they were no more.
> [Matt. 2:18]

Who is Jesus, the victorious Christ, in relationship to the unspeakable suffering of his own ancestors? The words of Jeremiah 31:15 evoke painful memories of earlier times of grief and exile with which the Savior is personally identified. Even the tragic massacre of children becomes the context for announcing life's victory.

> "But in truth, I tell you, there were many widows in
> Israel in the days of Elijah, when the heaven was shut
> up three years and six months, when there came a
> great famine over all the land; and Elijah was sent to
> none of them but only to Zarapeth, in the land of
> Sidon, to a woman who was a widow. And there were

> many lepers in Israel in the time of the prophet
> Elisha; and none of them was cleansed, but only
> Naaman the Syrian." When they heard this, all in the
> synagogue were filled with wrath.   [Luke 4:25–28]

Jesus had returned to his hometown of Nazareth, where he proclaimed, "The Spirit of the Lord is upon me, because he has anointed me to preach good news to the poor . . ." (Luke 4:18 ff.). The people responded with so much rejection and unbelief that even Jesus marveled (Mark 6:6). He reminded them of God's historical predisposition to the foreigner, the enemy, those outside the inner circle; and he left because "he could do no mighty work there" (Mark 6:5a). The message of God's victory was available to all, yet frequently it was met with rejection by insiders and acceptance by those outside.

> The Samaritan woman said to him, "How is it that
> you, a Jew, ask a drink of me, a woman of Samaria?"
> For Jews have no dealings with Samaritans. Jesus
> answered her, "If you knew the gift of God, and who
> it is that is saying to you, 'Give me a drink,' you
> would have asked him, and he would have given you
> living water."   [John 4:9–10]

Had he been a proper Jew, he would have avoided a hated Samaritan, and as a self-respecting rabbi, he would not have spoken publicly to a woman.[3] Yet Jesus witnessed to a new order in which all persons are equal before God. The Samaritan woman became the first person in the Gospel of John to whom the Lord revealed his messiahship, and she responded as an evangel to her family and community.

One paradox after another. The message—and the messenger—always proclaimed the good tidings. However, the circumstances and persons frequently were of an unexpected nature: Good news from a simple ordinary place; good news in the midst of utter tragedy; good news for those outside and in spite of rejection; good news for the hated and the oppressed. This was victorious good news indeed.

God was in Christ Jesus proclaiming the good tidings of

the victory of life over all forms of death. We look at the empty cross, so popular with Protestants, and are reminded of the resurrection victory demonstrated Easter day. All too easily we forget the Gethsemane struggle, the disciples' betrayal, the suffering of Good Friday, those earlier Holy Week events, which, like the anguished crucifix, also characterize the daily proclamation of Jesus' life. Consistent with Deutero-Isaiah, Jesus did not merely announce the reign of God's power; he actuated it. Bringing life into conflict with death meant struggle, suffering, rejection. Nevertheless, the proclamation went forth.

Describing how the church pursued her Lord's proclamation of victory for the next two millennia is a historical task undertaken by many writers. Within the last two decades, however, the church in America has experienced the emergence of an understanding of evangelism which differs from the above scriptural context. It appears less inspired by our Judeo-Christian heritage than by the phenomenon of church membership decline.

The golden 1950s witnessed the numerical and financial zenith of traditional churches in twentieth-century America. These years were followed by the social, political, racial, and economic struggles of the 1960s, which were paralleled by a radical shift from traditional church popularity.[4] Membership decreases continued through the 1970s, and only at the dawn of 1980 is there an apparent bottoming out of this trend. During the last two decades evangelism has been on the increase as a conscious program of the church. Its major thrust has been one of membership recruitment, to the extent that the terms *evangelism* and *church growth* have become synonymous.[5]

To be sure, the preaching of the gospel or proclamation of the good news in the New Testament accounts effected significant positive results (see Luke 4:22 and Acts 8:4 ff.) and even increases in adherents to the faith (note especially Acts 2:41, 6:7, 8:35 ff., 10:34–48, 11:20–21, and 14:21). But is the worth of the church to be found only in numerical growth? And when we discover our membership sagging, do we maintain the integrity of the gospel when we evangelize in order to rebuild our roster or expand it? In such a situation proclamation no longer results from joy over God's victory; it becomes a process by which the church handles its survival needs. And while survival in itself is not wrong, God calls the church not to see to its own survival but to serve.

I am reminded of two major events in the early 1970s in which I was involved. "A Celebration of Evangelism," sponsored by a pan-Presbyterian group, was held in Cincinnati in 1971 and again in Dallas in 1972. At the time I was a seminarian eager to learn what was going on in the church. I was asked to serve on the planning committee for the 1972 event designed to provide leadership training for laity and clergy throughout the various Presbyterian churches, whose memberships are 50 percent women and are generally smaller than two hundred members. Yet leadership primarily reflected male clergy of large congregations. Workshops offered various models for evangelism, invariably reflecting programs regarded as successful in terms of size and attractiveness. Both years there was a strong charismatic emphasis that the wind of the Spirit was at work in the celebration, yet I felt there was extensive manipulation in both the planning and the process.

This manipulation, as I experienced it, incorporated mixed signals. On the one hand pains were taken to include me on the planning committee: payment of expenses for all meetings, inclusion in all basic correspondence, and gracious personal reception by the others. On the other hand I recall a feeling of not being taken quite seriously. The only task given to me was to assist in the worship at one of our planning committee meetings. I did suggest a workshop on the ministry of women, both clergy and laity, but the counsel I received was that an undesirable narrowness would be conveyed if an ordained woman were to give it leadership, and the matter was dropped. My frustration must have heightened, for the one clear memory I still have is that at the opening of the conference I was permitted to be one of several persons to "log in" before the crowd of five hundred. Giving my minority report was probably one of my healthier personal experiences of handling conflict within the church. Manipulation by a process of inclusiveness (sometimes called tokenism) and limitation (or "invisibiliz-ing," as I have subsequently come to know it) has little to do with either the "wind of the Spirit" or with the stated first goal of the event: to experience the full meaning of evangel-ism.

This experience, as well as a number of other forms of gimmickry often found in activities associated with evangel-istic efforts, has served to leave me with a suspicious regard for the big numbers and success image of Madison Avenue-style outreach. For example, some evangelistic preachers lure donations with various kinds of promises or induce decisions for Christ by having counselors first come forward to an altar call. Lay evangelism is a very valuable activity which can be abused if a lifestyle of faithful service is replaced by learning to articulate faith through the recital of pat words and phrases. Sophisticated industry (the multi-million-dollar "electronic church") and simplistic media (bumperstickers preaching "Jesus Is My Co-pilot," "I Found It," "Honk if You Love Jesus") alike are pressed into service. The term *evangelism* has come to connote nonfaith values like survival, financial viability, success, and salesmanship more than it has good news.

Although the New Testament records occasions in which the proclamation of the gospel was received favorably and resulted in multiplied numbers, a sense of balance and wholeness is achieved when we also recognize that on a number of occasions the message/messenger experienced painful consequences. John the Baptizer, evangel of the Lord's own self, was imprisoned and capriciously beheaded. Our Lord was received well until he was heard to interpret Scripture fully and faithfully (see Luke 4:16–30). The experi-ence of Stephen is also a grim and striking reminder of the power and authority of God's witness through the evangel (see Acts 6 and 7).

God's sovereignty remains, yet here is reflected the hu-man condition into which the evangel or messenger of God is sent. Evangelism is the sending of the good news, not the anticipated response. The response may be good or bad or even indifferent, but it is not the task of the evangel to reckon the desired response and then design a form of the message simply to tell the listeners what they want to hear. This is manipulation, based on a consumer-oriented model. The church's true task is to witness faithfully.

Our congregation has been struggling to discover what it means to be faithful in this place at this time. In our first two years as pastors my husband and I shepherded the flock in established programs and patterns. Only then did it begin to come clear that the traditional forms were not necessarily compatible with current faithfulness. Session committees were alive and well although moving along in various directions. The budget and mission giving continually increased. But membership was slowly declining, and the church school was floundering, with low and erratic attendance. After study and evaluation it appeared that feelings that we were to blame were unmerited. Neighborhood schools were closing because of decreasing elementary-age population, and other traditional churches were not only watching their church school classes shrink but were closing altogether as a result of very limited community support. To persevere in making the old graded church school class system work where it did not fit the need seemed truly a waste of energy. Waste also accompanied the multidirectional efforts of the various programs in the church. Session committees, church school, youth groups, Sunday worship services—all were unrelated, sending out a confusion of philosophies, theologies, and interpretations. The message that the church projected to those inside and outside was mixed.

We began to look at the whole program of the church as having three basic divisions—worship, mission, and nurture—which are interrelated and mutually supportive. Worship is primary, for here we respond to God with adoration and praise, listen to God's word, and receive the impetus to go out and serve God in the world. Mission, or evangelism, is the going out in various forms of ministry, which both emanates from and returns to feed the worship. Nurture, or education, derives from and informs both worship and mission as the faithful grow in maturity in Christ. And thereby the work of the church becomes integrated.

How, then, to integrate the persons within the family of the church? All around us society erects barriers between ages and conditions. The eighty-year-old widow and the eight-year-old Little Leaguer rarely meet; young single career man and middle-aged man in wheelchair infrequently share experiences; professional mother of thirty-five, aspiring Hispanic woman student, and preschool Vietnamese girl—who live in the same neighborhood and share a common, changing feminine experience—may never relate personally. Such diversity and segmentation are especially characteristic of southern California, where the wholeness of life is lost in the cracks.

In response the session designed a new program built around the three emphases of worship, mission, and nurture. The program is scheduled quarterly in three- to six-week units in order to maximize the limited and varied times people have available. Each unit is intergenerational, inclusive, and unified thematically. Themes for this year have included worship, experiencing our history, world hunger and lifestyles, summer Sunday cinema series, and the Presbyterian mind. The result of the change is twenty-one weeks annually of integrated, focused, learning.

And what becomes of evangelism? As a committee of the session, it was dissolved because the whole life and work of the church is declaring the good news. Every Sunday one of the most significant parts of the worship is the sharing of prayer concerns. A brother asks prayerful support for his sister in her doctoral exams; another person reports that after a long near-death struggle with cancer his body is now found to be totally clean; a nurse is concerned for the one-and-one-half pound infant struggling for life in her neonatal ward; a political conservative confesses to un-Christlike resentment toward the Iranians, whom he realizes are also God-fearing; new grandparents thankfully announce the healthy arrival of "the most beautiful baby in the world"; continuing prayers are requested for all who surround a terminally ill loved one; and prayers are raised for the church in struggling Third World areas. Deep feelings of pain, perplexity, and joy characterize our prayerful life together and the Life within.

The church is evangel (*mebaser*), the messenger of God's victory. In recent history the church has perceived the message-bearing function in preponderantly masculine managerial imagery, commonly describing its activities in terms such as determining purpose, setting goals, enumerating resources, designing strategies, establishing measurements, and making evaluations. Some or all of these functions are frequently brought to serve the evangelistic task. But they not only serve, they also can affect the nature of the message itself. Such an external process can become abusive in its manipulation and domination unless it is tempered with an internal process of vulnerability. Let us investigate the alternative feminine imagery as a helpful complementary understanding of evangelism.

If the church is considered to be the bride of Christ, certainly it is appropriate to extend that biblical analogy and to describe her functions in more feminine terms (Jer. 2:2, 32; Eph. 5:23; Rev. 19:7; 21:2, 9; 22:17). In so doing, I clearly do not intend to regard the church as a place less for men than for women. It is a place equally for women and men. Further, in attempting to understand God and the life to which God calls people, we are constantly dealing with mysteries beyond our comprehension. Creation and all of its elements were provided not only as a witness to God's own self but also as means for our understanding, that those who have eyes to see and ears to hear might do so. This is the context which opens and guides my developing perceptions as a woman doing theology.

In this regard I should add that specific sex-identifiable language for God is not a major issue for me. I frequently speak of God as father (as Jesus certainly did), while attempting to emphasize non-sex-restrictive names of attributes such as Almighty, Lord, and Creator. However, in describing God I freely include the female nature and activity. God is like a mother in having given birth to all living creatures (Gen. 1; Isa. 51:1; Deut. 32:18). Sustenance is likewise a maternal behavior of God, as reflected in Genesis 1:29–30; Deuteronomy 32:11–12; Psalms 57:1 and 131:2; Isaiah 31:5, 46:3,

49:14–15; and Matthew 23:37. The mutuality of complementary roles (sexual and other) is reflected with great strength in the helper nature of Eve (Gen. 2:18–20), a role shared by God (Deut. 33:29; Pss. 33:20, 42:5, 46:1, 121:1, 124:8; and Acts 26:22.)[6]

These images and descriptions, however, must not serve as some kind of limits to God, by which I can claim her for my gender. But they do give me a clue that I am included in the message of good news, and they lead me beyond my human perception of life as either and only feminine or masculine. Since we are one sex or the other, I suspect that part of our human sexual crisis has resulted, in part, from a societal tendency to insist on clear sexual differentiation, not allowing for the wide range of shared masculine-feminine qualities within an individual. To neuterize would leave only an asexual world in which we would have even greater difficulty identifying selfhood and function. I hope that women's (and men's) liberation will help us regain a healthier regard for the interrelationship and complementary natures of female and male.

How, then, may the church regard herself as the evangel of God? The bride, as the womanlike body of Christ in the world, is regularly reminded that she was designed for the giving of life. Even a woman who has never conceived or given birth has no doubts about this aspect of her nature. The ability to birth may be used, abused, or unused. Nevertheless, its reality undeniably affects a woman's whole being. "It is not for you to know the seasons. . . . But you shall receive power when the Holy Spirit has come upon you; and you shall be my witness . . . to the end of the earth" (Acts 1:7–8; compare Luke 1:13–19, 35; Isa. 44:2, 49:1–5; and Jer. 1:5). The church, like her prototype Israel, was formed to bear the witness to God. Her message was the precious life placed within her. That life has been consistently characterized by the term *Word*, the effective presence of God. "And the Word became flesh and dwelt among us, full of grace and truth; we have beheld his glory . . ." (John 1:14).

The church has generally seen her task to be one of continuing the ministry of this Word, Jesus the Christ. But it is

also appropriate that she see herself as continuing the ministry as characterized by his mother, Mary. Called to be the
handmaid of the Lord (Luke 1:38), she served as one literally
filled with the Word of God. She was bursting with the good
news of the victory. If the church were to overly identify
with our Lord Jesus, fully born and fully matured, she might
be tempted to regard the Kingdom as having already fully
come. This postpartum concept is frustrated by the already-
but-not-yet nature of the daily life we experience; for in ac-
tuality the Kingdom of God has not fully come.

If, by contrast, the church were to identify with Mary—
full of the joy of expectation, burdened with her fullness,
and anxious as she approached the pain and uncertainties of
delivery—she might be given the grace to better see her present calling.

> We know that the whole creation has been groaning
> in travail together until now; and not only the
> creation, but we ourselves, who have the first fruits of
> the Spirit, groan inwardly as we wait for adoption. . . .
> For the creation waits with eager longing for the
> revealing of the [children] of God.
>
> [Rom. 8:22–23, 19]

As all of Jerusalem awaited the return of the exiles from Bab-
ylon, and their imminent arrival was heralded by the evangel who proclaimed, "Yahweh is King!" so the church awaits
the return of her Christ, and by her fullness of his presence
and hope she proclaims the victory of her Lord, mighty in
battle (Ps. 24:8).

As we look at the imagery of childbearing as an analogy
for the church, one further aspect is worth exploring. In the
anticipation and reception of a new life into a family, a problem frequently develops when the focus of the mother's af-
fection is redirected from the husband to the child. Many a
new father has felt abandoned by his wife's love, which, like
her time, can so easily be unwittingly transferred to the
newborn child. Preparatory to the birth, considerable time is
often spent painting, decorating, furnishing the nursery of
the house, readying the physical surroundings. Wise parents

know that a more than equal emphasis must be made in developing the relationship between themselves during both the preparation for and the care of the new family member. The health of a family depends in large measure on the soundness of the primary relationship of husband and wife. The church, the bride of Christ, in her eagerness to proclaim the good news to others, must never lose her central calling—to love God, with heart, soul, mind (Matt. 22:37). In the letter to the church at Ephesus, Jesus, through John, admonishes, ". . . you have abandoned the love you had at first" (Rev. 2:4). As important as a new birth certainly is, as important as the church's evangelistic task of bringing the new life of the gospel into the world is, it remains only one aspect of her calling. First, "You shall love the Lord your God," and second, "You shall love your neighbor . . ." (Matt. 22:37–39). The deep mutual love between the church and God is the greatest source of nourishment for the life within the church.

But the Lord's own self is the true Evangel, and the church as she bears the message of victory must also allow that message to speak to her.

> The Spirit of the Lord is upon me, because
> he has anointed me to preach good news to the poor.
> He has sent me to proclaim release to the captives
> and recovering of sight to the blind,
> to set at liberty those who are oppressed,
> to proclaim the acceptable year of the Lord.
>
> [Luke 4:18–19]

The church must yet fully claim her riches and release, her sight and freedom. We the evangels of Christ become the evangelized of Christ, thus witnessing to the wholeness of life God has given.

In the story that opened this chapter the congregation came alive through the witness of our unborn child. I, too, came alive in a way I could never have imagined. Like Mary, I was burdened with fullness and very anxious in anticipation of the uncertainties and pain of delivery, yet there is no denying the unspeakable wonder of being full of new life.

Like a mother, the church can embody the wisdom of Romans 8:18—that the pain endured and the possibility of death that always accompanies birth are not to be compared with the victory of life.

Notes

1. Gerhard Kittel, ed., *Theological Dictionary of the New Testament* (Grand Rapids, Mich.: Wm. B. Eerdmans, 1964), vol. II, pp. 707 ff.

2. See two books by James A. Sanders—*Torah and Canon* (Philadelphia: Fortress Press, 1972) and *God Has a Story Too* (Philadelphia: Fortress Press, 1979).

3. Raymond E. Brown, *The Gospel According to John I–XII* (Garden City, New York: Doubleday Anchor, 1966), pp. 170 ff.

4. For a study of this issue in the United Presbyterian Church see "A Summary Report of the Committee on Membership Trends," approved by the 188th General Assembly in 1976. Denominational offices are in New York City.

5. An example of church growth evangelism enjoying current popularity in some circles comes from the School of World Mission at Fuller Theological Seminary and is reflected in a new book by C. Peter Wagner, *Our Kind of People: The Ethical Dimensions of Church Growth in America* (Richmond, Va.: John Knox Press, 1979).

6. See Letty M. Russell, *Human Liberation in a Feminist Perspective—A Theology* (Philadelphia: Westminster Press, 1974), pp. 93–103.

UNBOXING CHRISTIAN EDUCATION

Martha Graybeal Rowlett

I was thirteen years old the summer I decided to go into the ministry. At a summer youth assembly I saw clearly the glory of the church's mission in the world, and with youthful idealism I decided to commit my life to that mission. This was a high and holy moment in my life. I heard the call to be in ministry in the church, and I answered it.

Because I was female, it was fairly simple to decide what kind of ministry that would be. There were a few women pastoring small churches, but full ordination was not yet possible for women in the Methodist Church. Opportunities there were severely limited: I could choose between being a

The Rev. Martha Graybeal Rowlett is currently enrolled in the Doctor of Ministry program of the School of Theology at Claremont in California. She has served United Methodist churches in Palo Alto, California, and Seattle. She holds degrees from Candler School of Theology and Pacific School of Religion. Prior to entering the ordained ministry she was a director of Christian education and served on the program staff of the California-Nevada Conference of the United Methodist Church.

missionary or being a director of Christian education. I had seen pictures of missionaries and had met a few, but that life seemed remote. My sense of call was to the local parish in this country. All my models for women in local church-related vocations were directors of Christian education. So I prepared to be a director of Christian education without seriously considering any alternatives.

When I started seminary in 1957, career opportunities in the ministry of Christian education looked good. Sunday schools were thriving, and almost every church had an active youth program. Churches were standing in line to hire Christian educators as the seminaries graduated them.

There was an aliveness about the Christian education program of the church that made it an exciting place to be. Vacation church schools, summer camps, youth prayer breakfasts, retreats, family life programs, laboratory schools, Christian workers' schools kept me busy from early morning to late night. People taught Sunday school classes and counseled youth groups sometimes for years, finding a kind of lay vocation. The future of Christian education looked bright.

From the beginning I enjoyed my work. Planning meetings with teams of teachers left me high from the stimulus of creativity sparking from person to person. The challenge of teaching pushed people to struggle through to a new level of Christian self-awareness. I was there as support and resource. I enlisted people to work in Christian education with the honest offer, "If you want to grow as a Christian yourself, then join a teaching team." I drew a lot of satisfaction from seeing children and young people—from babies through the teens—come to church knowing that they had a place there, that someone was prepared and waiting for them, that they belonged among the people of God. I enjoyed watching the program of Christian education grow, drawing more people into the Christian community.

But there were also undeniable reasons for professional dissatisfaction and frustration. These negative feelings, which in fact began in seminary, had to do with the sexism evident in the way the church structured the position of director of Christian education.

When I entered seminary, a small minority of the students were women, and all the women were in the Christian education program. Our curriculum was narrowly limited to educational methodology and curriculum resources. The degree program took only four quarters to complete, so there was little time for courses in Bible, church history, theology—the classical disciplines. Christian education was a kind of sideshow to the main production. Theoretical guidelines came more from the social sciences than from the nature of the faith. I felt boxed into a narrow space and shut out of the mainstream of seminary life.

In the local parish, although I was technically responsible for the educational ministry to all ages, I found that the adults of the church did not feel the need for my services. Their classes functioned as independent, small, lay-led congregations within the larger congregation. I was expected to work with the leaders of the children and youth, and that was it. Again, I felt boxed into a limited space and cut off from the mainstream of the church's life.

A second source of frustration was the status given to my ministry. The director of Christian education in most churches was the last hired and the first fired. The salary was often scarcely half that of the pastor. Benefits were limited, and there was no pension plan. Christian education was considered to be "women's work" and had second-class rank in the church.

This was not what I had envisioned at thirteen. But this was where the professional services of women were welcomed and employed by the church at that time.

Lyle Schaller, in his book *The Multiple Staff and the Larger Church*,[1] divides the tasks of ministry in the local church into two groups, the "winners" and the "losers," on the basis of status and job satisfaction. "Winners" include preaching, hospital calling, teaching, conducting weddings and funerals. Christian education is one of the "losers." Schaller perceives Christian education as a low-visibility, low-status, behind-the-scenes staff function. For example, rarely does the senior minister on a multiple staff carry responsibility for the Christian education program. Schaller concludes by warning that professional staff members limited to "loser" ministries ultimately will experience frustration. And I did.

My joy in my ministry was clouded by feelings of being artificially isolated in a specialization that was considered neither central nor essential in the life of the church.

My sense of professional frustration was compounded by the fact that during the 1960s the Christian education box began to shrink. By this time I was on a regional denominational staff, and my job included leadership training for Christian educators and church leaders in two states. Without warning Sunday school membership and attendance in the mainline Protestant churches began to decline. New curricula and special promotions awakened hope, introduced some needed reforms, but failed to turn the tide. With an increase in the number of women working outside the home, volunteers to staff educational programs became increasingly difficult to enlist and train. People wanted to work short-term shifts as class leaders; they no longer had time for the week-long leadership training programs that had flourished just a few years earlier.

From my regional post I watched creative people try a wide range of innovations in Christian education. Weekday classes, contract classes for regular attenders, learning center approaches to teaching, and intergenerational settings were heralded as solutions to the attendance problem. But each year the overall statistics for participation in Christian education continued to decline. The picture was not totally dark: Sunday schools were still influencing the lives of millions of people. Many churches continued to have active youth programs. New forms of adult education were having some success. Lay teachers were still exercising their ministries, some very effectively. But the trend in participation was unmistakably downward.

Several denominations, reading the signs of the times, went through bureaucratic restructuring. Many long-term Christian educators lost employment as their positions were eliminated. This happened to me; the staff on which I served was reduced from seven specialists to two generalists.

Ordination for women had been possible in the United Methodist Church since 1956, although few women had taken advantage of the opportunity. At this crisis point in my professional ministry I decided to move from being a specialist in Christian education to being a generalist in Christian ministry. That meant a second trip to seminary, this time for a master of divinity degree.

When I landed on campus, I discovered another trend of the times. While Sunday school attendance had been going down, the number of women attending seminary had begun to go up. No longer were these women registering only for degrees in Christian education. From a small percentage hardly sufficient to merit the use of inclusive language in the seminary classroom, women very quickly came to make up from one-quarter to one-third of the student body. And most of them were headed for the ordained ministry. I discovered that women were climbing out of the Christian education box. They were talking about being pastors and chaplains, about tackling all the varieties of ministries that the church offers. And because of the long history of being limited to Christian education jobs, many of the women stoutly resisted any identification at all with the educational ministry of the church. There was a kind of reaction against doing "women's work" any longer.

Meanwhile, Christian education had shifted from being a female preserve. The profession of director of Christian education was created originally by and for men, but the Depression of the 1930s had forced the salaries down and lowered the status of the job, resulting in a retreat of men from the job and an influx of women. For four decades women had dominated the profession. But in the 1970s this trend was being reversed again. By 1979 the membership of the Christian Educator's Fellowship of the United Methodist Church was 40 percent men and 60 percent women.

Church-related vocations, it appeared, were finally being determined by gifts and interests rather than by sex.

A major breakthrough had been made in the roles of women in professional ministry in the United Methodist Church. We were free to be specialists or generalists, lay or ordained, as our call and our circumstances indicated. We could offer professional leadership in every dimension and on every level of the church's life. No longer would Christian education be equated with "women's work."

No such radical change occurred in the way the churches did Christian education, however. The Sunday school continued to be the single most popular program. In 1980 the Sunday school was 200 years old. Started as a lay movement outside the church, it had become part of the church, powerfully influencing Christian education. Commentators note much to celebrate in this history. Millions of people have been introduced to the Bible story in Sunday school. Devout lay people have witnessed to their faith and have shared their struggle to be true to the Christian faith in their places of work and in their homes. People of all ages have learned passages of Scripture and verses of songs that they later recalled in prisoner-of-war camps and on hospital beds to provide the sustaining power of faith. They experienced real caring in the classes where an absence elicited a postcard and any serious problem was a matter of shared concern. They contributed to projects to meet human need both near and far away, and in the process learned generosity. There was much to be said for the contributions of the Sunday school.

But the birthday was also the occasion for a wide mixture of prophecies about the future of the Sunday school. Sunday school enrollment in the United States, already slipping badly in the late 1960s, dropped from just over 40 million in 1970 to 32 million in 1979.[2] Commemorating the bicentennial, Martin Marty referred to the Sunday school as a "battered survivor," noting that such alternatives as religion in the public schools and weekday religious education had failed to survive as long.[3] D. Campbell Wyckoff offered hope for the Sunday school's continued serviceability. He compared it to crabgrass, suggesting that while it leaves much to be desired, it does meet a need, and alternatives are much more trouble than they are worth.[4] John Westerhoff, on the other hand, took a radical position and declared that he could see no significant role for the Sunday school in the church of the future. He has committed himself to search for alternatives.[5]

The foundations of what has been in Christian education

in recent history are being shaken. What is to be is not yet clear.

One thing is clear to me, however. I have changed my identity from "professional Christian educator" to "parish minister"—but I have not stopped doing Christian education. I have simply broadened the context to the whole life of the church and expanded my leadership style from "enabler" to include "doer."

It seems to me that the commission to teach the gospel is clearly part of the responsibility of the ordained clergy. It is not a lay prerogative. Clergy are called to be teachers as well as preachers, priests, pastors. Christian education is the job of the whole church, and I am still doing it.

How do I *do* Christian education as a parish minister? When there is no director of Christian education on the staff, I continue to do many of the things I did in that job, enlisting, training, and supporting lay teachers, counselors, and group leaders. With an education professional on the staff, I share team responsibility for that work. But I do more. I preach. I design worship. I administer the sacraments. I teach. I counsel people with problems. I visit the sick and people in crisis. I share the mission of the church to the world. I try to draw new people into the church. In all of these activities I am involved in Christian education.

Christian education has been defined in many ways. It is the church's commission, "Go and teach all nations." It is the process of nurturing, informing, equipping, and training members for ministry. It is "equipping the saints for the work of ministry, for building up the body of Christ" (Eph. 4:12).

John Westerhoff describes Christian education as centering in a story, the story of God's relationship with the world. The goal of Christian education, he says, is that people might know, understand, own, and live that story as their own. This doesn't happen only when a person is involved in an experience in the church that is clearly defined as educational. Ideally, people are confronted by the story and invited to make a personal response by everything that the church is and does and says.[6]

If we accept Westerhoff's definition, the implication is

that almost everything we do in the church can be Christian education.

In my first parish assignment I approached all of my ministry with an educational perspective. I had learned as an educator to "start where the people are." So in my preaching, for example, I tried to relate the gospel message to where the people were. My first congregation was in Palo Alto, California, a sophisticated, well-to-do suburb of San Francisco. I listened to what the people talked about. I kept up with current events and noted what books they were reading and what films they were seeing. I tried to create sermons in dialogue with what I perceived they were thinking and feeling.

My second parish was in Des Moines, Washington, a suburb of Seattle. There I adopted a style of preaching that begins with the text and then relates it to life. In preparing a sermon, I ask myself where God encounters the human situation in the passage on which I am working. I look for human problems and concerns that may be illumined by the passage and for insights into our specific contemporary situation. I ask myself, "How would our lives change if we believed this and acted on it?" Then I share the gospel story from the pulpit, calling for a response of commitment to the story as the people's own story.

I also believe that in designing and leading worship services and administering the sacraments, I am involved in Christian education. People learn by doing, I had been taught as an educator. In the worship experience people learn a lot of theology. As I design and lead a worship service, I am telling the story; I am involving people in the sharing of that story. One of the joys of the ministry for me has been working with other staff and lay people to design worship services for the seasons of the church year. We have experienced the longing for the coming of a savior as we have lighted the candles on the Advent wreath. We have shared together the joy and wonder of the Incarnation as we have reenacted the Christmas story. We have dramatized the spread of the church by lighting candles from the Christ candle and spreading the light through the congregation on

Epiphany. We have stood at the foot of the cross as we remembered the last words of Christ on Good Friday. We have recalled his lonely death as we have extinguished the candles in a Tenebrae service. We have celebrated the Resurrection on Easter and the birth of the church on Pentecost with songs and brass instruments and balloons and banners. In baptism we have claimed as our own the story of the gracious welcome of undeserving humanity into God's family. In the Lord's Supper we have celebrated the continuing nurturing presence of the crucified and risen Christ among us. On every Sunday we have praised, confessed, made our needs and desires known to God, and listened for and responded to God's word to us. It seems to me that in a well-rounded and vital worship program we do some of our best Christian education.

Another way in which I do Christian education as a parish minister is by teaching. As a director of Christian education, my job was to enable the teaching ministry of other people; my own teaching was limited primarily to leadership development settings. As a pastor, I am welcome, indeed expected, to be a teacher of Scripture, doctrine, and heritage. Most of what I have done has been in adult education, leading small groups and classes and retreats and workshops on the Bible, prayer, Christian doctrines, the history of Methodism, the meaning of the sacraments, and Christian lifestyle issues. I have also taught confirmation classes for young people, introducing them to the story and to what it means to respond with the commitment of discipleship. And I have been "guest teacher" with children's classes, introducing them to the sacraments and talking to them about what the minister does. Leadership development is also a teaching role. I have trained leaders in classes on group dynamics and workshops on church organization. But most of my teaching is on a one-to-one basis as I help a lay person understand what he or she needs to do and how it might be done. Often this is the point where a person is helped to move beyond hearing and understanding the gospel story to owning and living it in and through the church.

Pastoral counseling provides another opportunity for

Christian education. After my ordination I was startled at how quickly people opened up and shared deeply personal things with me. It was as if I suddenly had a brand-new avenue into peoples' lives. In this role I had become someone they could trust with their real feelings. Often all they needed was someone to listen and help them sort out what was going on, to get a fresh perspective on a problem. But at times there was a need for something more, for spiritual direction, for ethical guidance. So a kind of one-to-one Christian education took place. "Will God punish me for having an abortion?" "I'm so depressed that I am thinking about suicide." "I don't understand why God let my child die." These have all been starting places for the sharing of the story.

The mission projects of the church are tools of Christian education. People learn more by what we are and do than by what we say, I learned as an educator. Both congregations that I have served have resettled refugee families, guiding and supporting them through the process of adjustment to this country. Whole families worked together. Children shared their toys and helped entertain the refugee children. Young people helped with language tutoring. All ages pitched in to get the job done, and by doing this they were involved in intergenerational Christian education. The California congregation provides delicious, nutritional meals at low cost for senior citizens on fixed incomes. The people who cooked, served, entertained, and cleaned up were telling the story, owning and living it. The Washington congregation supports a medical mission to Haiti, raising money and collecting eyeglasses to help an ophthalmologist who works in one of the poorest nations in the Western Hemisphere. They are living and telling the story. In both churches I have worked with committees that reflected respect and caring for each of their individual members in the way they worked. I experienced this respect and caring as a witness to the story. Even in compiling budget requests and in raising the church budget, I have felt myself to be still a Christian educator.

I am involved in Christian education when I visit a new family in town and invite them to be part of our church. As I interpret the church and its life and what it can mean to them, I am telling them the story and inviting them to make it their own story. The invitation to come and follow Christ is the first step in disciple formation.

Christian education goes on when I minister to people in crisis situations: at the death of a family member; at the time of an accident, or serious illness or divorce, or trouble with the law, or unemployment. Crises often stimulate doubts that lead to questions never before asked. Shock sometimes breaks through barriers of self-satisfaction and creates openness to hearing the story in a fresh way and at new level of the personality. Few teachers have the opportunities that pastors have to relate their teaching to the life situation of the learner.

Christian education is one of the major and central functions of the Christian church. Something is wrong in the church when Christian education is boxed off and given second-class status, just as something is wrong when women are limited in their professional service to the church and when what they do is considered to be of secondary importance.

The church needs programs specifically designed to do Christian education, like the Sunday school. It needs age group and intergenerational groups. It needs the teaching ministry of the laity. It needs professionals who will specialize in Christian education.

But these are not enough. The whole ministry of the church is involved in Christian education.

And women have gifts and graces to bring to every aspect of that whole ministry. Perhaps as women come out of the Christian education box and find their place in the whole ministry of the church, we will see the walls of that box disappearing. Perhaps one of the by-products of the ordination of women will be a renewal of the church's ministry of Christian education, a renewed acknowledgment of its central postition in the mission of the church. Perhaps as women come into the ordained ministry, the clergy will take with new seriousness their ancient function as teacher in the congregation.

For the future we need a wholeness of humanity, men and women, lay and ordained, working together in a wholeness of ministry if the work of Christian education is to be done.

Notes

1. Lyle E. Schaller, *The Multiple Staff and the Larger Church,* (Nashville: Abingdon Press, 1980).

2. Figures from the Institute for American Church Growth, Pasadena, California, cited in the *United Methodist Reporter,* June 20, 1980.

3. Martin Marty, "The Sunday School: Battered Survivor," *The Christian Century,* June 4–11, 1980, p. 634.

4. D. Campbell Wyckoff, "As American as Crabgrass: The Protestant Sunday School," *Religious Education,* Jan.–Feb. 1980, p. 27.

5. John H. Westerhoff, III, "The Sunday School of Tomorrow," *The Christian Century,* June 4–11, 1980, p. 641.

6. John H. Westerhoff, III, *Will Our Children Have Faith?* (New York: Seabury Press, 1976), p. 34.

THE
EMBODIED
CHURCH

Lora Gross

He spoke very little English when he walked across
the border of his native Mexico. He speaks very little
now. He had no relatives in the United States. He
was twenty-one, unskilled. His family was very poor.
He had no job. He crossed the border illegally into
what he hoped would be the land of opportunity. It
wasn't. He traveled cheaply—mostly on freight trains.
His journey ended beneath the wheels of one of those
trains in Nebraska. The accident claimed a portion of
his left leg. Doctors and staff members performed the
surgery and treatment his condition demanded. Immi-
gration and Naturalization agents were notified.

*The Rev. Lora Gross is co-pastor of Augustana Lutheran Church
and co-director of Lutheran Metropolitan Ministries in Omaha,
Nebraska. She began her ministry as a deaconess in the Lutheran
Church—Missouri Synod and later was ordained in the Lutheran
Church in America. She is a graduate of Valparaiso University and
the Lutheran School of Theology in Chicago.*

When he was well enough to travel, they said, he
would be deported.[1]

Davil Zaragoza is one of thousands of undocumented workers who have come to Omaha. Many are poor and are looking for work; most speak no English and have no relatives in
this country. Often they become victims of systems they do
not understand. There is a man in Omaha who cares about
such people—Alberto Rodriguez, once a migrant worker
himself. He heard about Davil and raised over a thousand
dollars in the community to fit him with an artificial limb,
pay his hospital expenses, and help pay tuition for him in a
vocational school in Mexico. Al works full time as a janitor,
and in his "spare time" he works for the church. Al is a
nominally paid staff worker for Lutheran Metropolitan Ministries in Omaha. His presence at Lutheran Metropolitan
Ministries and his work in the Hispanic community of south
Omaha are an outgrowth of the embodied church in social
ministry.

Metropolitan Ministries is where I spend a portion of my
days, too, as a minister of the Nebraska Synod of the Lutheran Church in America. It is a dual call to this social ministry agency and Augustana Lutheran Church, a 560-member
urban congregation in Omaha. I share both assignments
with the Rev. Victor Schoonover. We are now in our second
three-year term call.

Every day as we begin our work, we are confronted by the
harsh realities of urban life—poverty, racism, crime. All tear
deeply at the social fabric and challenge the church's rhetor-
ic of love, justice, and wholeness. As we've sought to define
our ministry in Omaha, I've found myself drawn to a query
by James Nelson whether there is an interconnection between human sexuality and the broken relationship among
human beings that is at the very roots of social injustice.[2] At
first, this seems like a rather startling thesis. As we conceive
of the mission of the church to the world, one of the last
things we think about is human sexuality. On what basis
would we attempt to understand ourselves as sexual beings

with the thought that it would give us a clue to the great social issues of our time?

Such a reaction is not surprising if you take a moment to examine our heritage. Early Christian writings were influenced by Greek thought, which held to a strict body-spirit dualism. Such a philosophy produces an alienation of spirit from body, or reason from emotion, the "higher life" from the "fleshly life." As a result, observes Nelson, "Our conceptual worlds become populated with dichotomies—me/not me, male/female, masculine/feminine, heterosexual/homosexual, black/white, smart/stupid, healthy/ill, good/bad, right/wrong."[3]

But if you place this analysis in juxtaposition with the *core* of the Christian gospel, you have yet another dilemma. The kernel out of which the gospel becomes the living Word among us is the Incarnation. "And the Word became *flesh* and dwelt among us . . ." (John 1:14). The Word is not just a cognitive, intangible expression of divine, static wisdom. The Word breathes and is fluid. The Word laughs, weeps, suffers, and celebrates resurrection. God came in human form in the historical Jesus. In this event body and spirit were molded into one inseparable identity. The Incarnation gives the church its wholeness; its ministry cannot be fragmented into spiritual and physical concerns. This identity gives the church its potency in the world. If we take seriously the incarnational principle, how can we participate in the dualism which is operative all around us and by which we so often are defined? It is through this dilemma that the church carves out its perspective of social ministry.

I want to suggest, then, that the church's social ministry is the embodiment of the gospel, which empowers human creatures in the world to be fully human and present to one another as women and men. The term *embodiment* means that as human beings we relate in the world not only as "doers" but as "be-ers." The term *embodiment* presumes a body-presence that is vital in my understanding of what it means for God to be incarnate in the world through me and you—the church. Further, the concept of embodiment speaks about the way I am present in my body, and that includes who I am as a sexual being. "To be" and "to do" in the world as a Christian, I need to recognize my femaleness and my maleness—my androgyny—as a vital indicator of what God is about in the world. And that primarily is relationship, God with us and us with one another.

An understanding of myself as body, then, is vital as I seek to understand my Christian responsibility to the world. Nelson talks about human sexuality as "a sign, a symbol, and a means of our call to communication and communion. . . . The mystery of our sexuality is the mystery of our need to reach out to embrace others both physically and spiritually. Sexuality thus expresses God's intention that we find our authentic humanness in relationship."[4] If I am to be a loving servant in the world, I need to know my capacity to love. And I cannot experience love in the fullest, richest sense as a disembodied presence, nor can others experience the extent of my loving without relating to me as a body-self. I think the church too often has sabotaged its ability to empower human lives by not fully understanding and honoring itself as fleshly presence. If social ministry comes down to what it means for women and men to be present in the world as fully human, then the power of actualizing whole and just relationships must come from a full understanding of the self not only as mind and spirit but as sexual body-presence as well.

Establishing the connection between issues of human sexuality and justice challenges the church's theology of social ministry in three ways. First, it challenges it to embrace a body-self presence in and to the world. Second, it challenges it to confront and transform abuses of patriarchal power, which is the undergirding of social injustice. Third, it challenges it to define, develop, and integrate an androgynous experience of empowerment for individuals and social institutions, including the church.

In meeting these challenges as the church, we can envision what could happen if we let ourselves fully know and feel our presence as androgynous, embodied people of God in the world. What kind of power would come from that kind of presence? What kind of potency would the church's presence have in the area of social justice? Would our traditional definition of power as potency earned through competition change to potency that is presence, a way of being in and with the world? Empowerment that comes in the freedom to express spontaneously to the world the embodied presence of the People of God is an authenic matrix for social ministry.[5] In empowering the world through the church's presence, we embody the only legitimate use of power available to us as Christians, namely, the incarnate presence of Christ. This premise calls for a discussion of power that exposes both its destructive use in the church and society and its unlimited possibilities for healing and wholeness when understood as embodied, androgynous presence.

The abuse of power, as I perceive it, is its identification with a patriarchal hold on the structure of society. Historically, patriarchy or patriarchal power has shaped most of the conceptual patterns, values, and customs of Western culture. One author defines patriarchal behavior as "cool and unemotional rather than warm and emotive, expedient rather than purposeless, aggressive rather than passive, unreflective rather than reflective. Patriarchal institutions tend to be ordered along hierarchical 'chain of command' or 'lines of authority' rather than being communal and anarchic; they are exclusive rather than inclusive and are goal directed rather than maintenance oriented."[6] A conscious or unconscious belief in the basic superiority of men and inferiority of women inevitably affects the convictions we hold about the meaning of community, about nature, the mission of the church to society, issues of justice, perceptions of God and the divine purpose. There is nothing original in this perception; the problem lies in understanding it in the chemistry of our thinking, our feeling, our relationships.

Disembodied presence is the death-dealing characteristic of a patriarchal system. Traditionally women have been defined solely by their biological functions and have been considered to possess inferior characteristics of mind and spirit. Men, on the other hand, have been characterized as possessing primarily the higher, superior attributes of spirit and mind. The norm for goodness, reality, and divinity has been clearly male. Inferior and evil attributes have long been associated with femaleness. What we have, then, in both the church and society, are subordinate female bodies and dominant disembodied males as a gender system which forms the basis for an entire social system. The injustice to women in such a patriarchal system is obvious, especially when we are identified as bodies within a structure that values only attributes of spirit and mind. The injustice is concretely realized in issues such as abortion, prostitution, pornography, rape, and wife abuse, among others.[7]

Lutheran Metropolitan Ministries works with community groups in Omaha that are addressing needs related to some of these issues. In my work with the Abused Women Shelter and as religious consultant to the YWCA's Rape Hot Line, it is clear to me that many people do not understand the root justice issue that gives rise to these crimes. Last year I went with a rape victim through the process of reporting the crime to the police, the grueling interrogation by the detectives, the long hospital examination, and finally the agony of being put on the bottom of a police priority list of rape cases. While most people involved in that process were helpful and not openly hostile, there was nevertheless a residue of distrust, embarrassment, and a casual attitude toward the rape victim. These attitudes indicate to me that the people involved in the process were not able to understand that this woman was the victim of a crime of power and violence and not a crime of sexual lust. I experienced further evidence of this gross misconception when a volunteer consulted me about a distraught rape victim who was told by her priest that she must go to confession and receive absolution for her sin in order to be right with God.

Another example of a crime against women which is a by-product of the patriarchal abuse of power in our society is wife abuse. The shelter in Omaha is forced weekly to turn away large numbers of abused women because they do not have the facilities to accommodate all the women who come for help. Many women who retreat to the shelter are abused repeatedly. I spoke with one about the circumstances of her most recent beating from her husband. She told me, "He said I should be glad he came home at all. He does bring home the paycheck so the kids and I can eat. I guess that makes it worth it."

In both rape and wife abuse, which are crimes of violence and power against women, several things are apparent. Men tend to view women and women tend to view themselves primarily as bodies and inferior to the hierarachy of the male power system, which is disembodied presence. In my experience, even when these acts are acknowledged as crimes, there seems to be a deep and pervading belief by both women and men, consciously or unconsciously, that the "natural order" of things gives a primitive permission to men to victimize women and for women to see themselves as victims. As a result, a sexual symbiosis develops in relationships, permitting the persecutor role for men and the victim role for women. It is interesting to note that statistics show that wife beating crosses all economic, racial, and cultural lines, and there is no one primary cause. The malady lies in the intrinsic sexism of our society and culture. While this sexual symbiosis is blatant in such crimes as wife abuse and rape, it also is evident within the dynamics of a variety of traditionally acceptable female-male relationships. Women experience victimization as the continual brunt of sexist jokes, exclusive language, and being thrust into child-parent communication patterns with men. In more subtle situations much of the abuse of patriarchal power may not be *legally* criminal, but the seeming intrinsic "rightness" of male superiority and female submissiveness is every bit as potent.

In the patriarchal system, with its hierarchy of power, women are left powerless. They are the prime victims in such a system. Ironically, however, men also become victims of the very system which names them superior and bestows on them the trappings of power. In the last decade, as women have begun to understand the injustice of a patriarchal power system, so men are beginning to realize the gross dehumanization of being disembodied creatures. Men are slaves to a system that tells them not to feel, only to think;

not to build warm, intimate relationships with women and children, only to control them; not to get close and experience the tender strength of another man, but to fear their own sexuality. There is deep suffering in a disembodied orientation to life. But the evils of patriarchy don't end with the dehumanization of the sexes. Patriarchal power becomes the core of a great variety of social injustices. Women, identified with the bodiness men have learned to despise in themselves, become paradigms of powerlessness for all other subjugated groups, classes, castes, and races.[8] Eldridge Cleaver puts it bluntly: "Only when the white man comes to respect his own body, to accept it as part of himself, will he be able to accept the black man's mind and treat him as something other than the living symbol of what he has rejected in himself."[9]

Further implications of disembodiment as the core issue of social injustice are seen in problems such as ecological abuse, the neglect of the elderly, and rejection of the handicapped from the "normal" flow of life.[10] If the church chooses to work within the world as a disembodied, patriarchal power, then it participates in the very structures that are the roots of social injustice. The church benefits by conceiving of social ministry as both "doing" and "being" in the world. There is power in the presence the church offers to society and to justice issues.

Embodying the gospel in a power system that disembodies itself to maintain and perpetuate institutionalized racism, sexism, and poverty is a major ongoing challenge for the church. Lutheran Metropolitan Ministries has attempted to meet part of that challenge by helping to develop a variety of community programs and projects. One such effort is a federally funded project to restore medical and dental services to a rapidly declining neighborhood in north Omaha. Metropolitan Ministries has been involved actively in fair housing issues such as scattered site housing and red lining in certain communities of the city. Our office has developed a presence in south Omaha among the large, rapidly growing Hispanic population. We sponsor a Lutheran Pantry and a free Indian and Chicano health clinic and support a bilingual resource coordinator in the community. These services meet some of the physical needs of the community through the concrete presence of the church.

An equally important issue of justice is the philosophy of community ministry by which Lutheran Metropolitan Ministries functions. Though our office sponsors, supports, and acts as consultant and advocate for these ministries, they are not directed by the Lutheran Metropolitan Ministries staff. As soon as community ministries are able to be self-sustaining, they are spun off from our office into the hands of community leadership. For example, the Low Income Women's Coalition was developed by low income women interested in helping other women and their children survive and improve their economic status. Breaking the poverty cycle, helping women see themselves as more than victims, and attracting community resources and support is an ongoing task for this group. The challenge of social ministry is to provide services while empowering the people being served. The embodied church works in opposition to patriarchal systems of power that dehumanize and discriminate through paternalism in the delivery of services in the inner city.

I like to use the verb *to empower* when speaking about the kind of power which has the capacity to fill up or to make strong rather than to dominate and to control or even to bestow, as in a patriarchal definition. Eleanor Haney calls this empowering presence *centering*. She uses the term to describe the method women are using to establish their own self-identity with other women as opposed to being identified with a man. This self-centering offers an end to hierarchical male power. Haney recognizes centering to be vital for women as a process of gaining autonomy, power, integration, consistency, and responsibility—namely, unique presence in the world.[11]

Lutheran Metropolitan Ministries has developed programs for women in church and community to build the kind of centering to which Haney refers. Ordained and lay women of the Lutheran Church in five states met in Omaha in 1977 for a three-day leadership conference entitled "Does

Power Have Gender?" In this experience several dynamics were evident. Though each woman was at a different point in her journey, all the women expressed a strong need for support in their work. Most women shared a general feeling of isolation and loneliness at work and a great hunger for authentic affiliation with other women. There seemed to be a balancing between the expression of a great deal of anguish and a deep, pervading sense of excitement and celebration. I find these two dynamics in almost every women's group I've been a part of in the last ten years. Female affiliation is vital to the growth of women as centered selves. Women need to be able to go to other women with pain and celebration as the journey through archaic power systems and identities derived through men continues.

The idea of a centered empowerment, which comes in valuing one's body-self, has interesting implications for social ministry. If patriarchal definitions of power are inadequate for women and men to integrate themselves as fully human, they also are inadequate for understanding the world. As self-centering is a starting point for women in attaining an identity, so it can offer a starting point for the church's relationship to society as embodied presence. For the church to be an embodied, empowered presence in the world, women and men need continually to explore what their individual presence is saying to themselves, each other, and society and the impact that presence is having on the social ministry of the church. In our patriarchal system, which seems intrinsic in Christian theology, church policy, and societal structures, we've been lopsided on the side of disembodied, male definitions of what it is to be human. So what I'm suggesting as the last component of a perspective on the church's social ministry is a discussion of androgyny, the union of masculine and feminine characteristics in one human personality.

I am finding in my own journey toward androgynous development that it is helpful to talk about androgyny as a process by which the tough (traditionally male) and the tender (traditionally female) begin to flow into one another in a toughly tender and/or tenderly tough presence that is uniquely me. I don't intend to propose that androgyny is a cure-all for the ailing dynamics between women and men or that it is the "salvation" for the church's social ministry. Still, if we accept the premise that the patriarchal power system disembodies people and renders women and men powerless, then androgyny is at least a necessary transitional concept pointing toward a more humanized way "to be" in the world as individuals and as the church. I envision an empowerment which comes through an embodied maleness and femaleness as a means by which we seek each other not as opposites but as sisters and brothers coming together as human neighbors, institutions, races, and cultures.

For instance, one of the most exciting experiences of working with my dual calling to the Augustana congregation and Lutheran Metropolitan Ministries is the continual contact with a variety of ethnic groups and cross-cultural experiences Through our various ministries the body needs of people are being served. Through the presence of the church in the community, women and men of a variety of cultural backgrounds experience the fleshly and spiritual attributes of the church's social ministry as their lives and communities are empowered. Augustana, which is a primarily Swedish congregation, sponsors a Laotian refugee family and provides space and facilities for a growing Indo-Chinese group that meets weekly. Augustana also participates in Project Embrace, a tutoring program for neighborhood school children. The administrative offices for Project Embrace are housed at Augustana, and many tutors and board members come from the congregation. The program also hires a worker from the community to direct a year-round recreational program for community youth of all ages. These activities are duplicated in five other urban sites in the inner city.

At Lutheran Metropolitan Ministries we have consultants from the black, Hispanic, native American, and low income white communities. Our female-male pastoral team further exemplifies an embodied social ministry; there is an empowering sense of world community among us. Although the economic, racial, and sexual barriers still reinforce old prejudices and stereotypes, the seeds of justice, equality, and unity of God's people in the world are sown and nurtured. There is power for the church's ministry in that kind of presence in the world. It is a presence the world can take hold of because it is embodied as flesh as well as spirit.

The church's sacramental life—the flesh and blood presence in the Eucharist and the naming and claiming of embodied people in baptism—compliments this perspective on its mission in the world. A holistic flow of femaleness and maleness is not something we have to add to ourselves as self-actualized persons; it is not a foreign reality to us because it is already a part of us. We simply need to accept the power to become what we are, namely, unique individuals, male and female, each with the capacity for both characteristics. The church need not be relegated in its presence to the world as mother church with father God. The church can be both female and male in presence as we draw from a God who also embodies the whole spectrum of human attributes. There is power in an equalitarian presence where the characteristics and values of neither traditional sex role are assumed superior to those of the other. The androgynous perspective calls for unity of self and gender values for women and men in just and whole relationships. The same embodied presence empowers the church and societal institutions as they work together for social justice.

Moving toward a holistic presence of women and men together and as unique individuals is a key issue of justice for the church and society. It is also an opportunity for the church, called to be embodied presence in the world, to conceive, labor with, and give birth to a more well-rounded concept of power as empowerment. In the struggle of the sexes to actualize whole and just relationships, I have observed in my own process, and in the process of other Christian women and men, three basic dynamics that I think would be helpful to explore here. The first dynamic is the traditional stance. The woman seeks personal power and identity derivatively through the man. I have diagrammed this dynamic as follows, using the term *powerless* to indicate the condition of patriarchy.

$$\text{POWERLESS WOMEN} \xrightarrow[\text{through}]{\text{identity}} \text{POWERLESS MEN}$$

Derivative identity is an easy mistake for women because the nature of the power sought is patriarchal, making the male the only access to that kind of power for the female. The problem in this dynamic is that both women and men are duped into believing patriarchy is empowerment, when in fact both female and male remain powerless.

The second dynamic occurs when women begin to center within their own experience and value themselves as body-selves in spite of the societal norm. When women reject patriarchal power as inhibiting to life-producing identity and begin to integrate their own femaleness and maleness, a certain kind of dangerous relationship can develop with some men, both personally and professionally. Female relationships with males who are still trapped in powerless definitions become derivative identity for the male through the female. I illustrate that dynamic in the following way:

$$\text{POWERLESS MEN} \xrightarrow[\text{through}]{\text{identity}} \text{EMPOWERED WOMEN}$$

This situation is dangerous to women who are developing their own identity for two reasons. First, the newfound empowerment can and does tend to attract powerless men, and second, the kind of symbiotic relationship which results can sap the woman's strength to continue to actualize herself in that particular relationship. The trap here is the deeply embedded gender role characteristics of women. Our strong nurturing qualities and our tendency to take responsibility for other people's lives can move us into a mother-son relationship with powerless men. This dynamic is similar to the one discussed above in that as women seek derivative identity from men, a father-daughter dynamic tends to develop. Both these types of female-male relationships are variations on the patriarchal power theme. However, the mother-son relationship may not always be apparent at first because the woman is seeking empowerment outside of the male. The powerless man seeks empowered identity through the woman instead of taking responsibility for his own development. Empowered women who permit this misuse of their body-self attributes soon find themselves in the same dominant-submissive power model of traditional patriarchy.

The third dynamic I find especially painful because it results in a block to sisterhood among women. The process of women centering in their own empowered identities outside of the male norm is often a slow and agonizing process for those desiring to make that journey. There are some women who will never choose to begin the move from derivative identity and patriarchal power structures. As women in all stages and states of identity development seek to affiliate, the tendency for powerless women is to seek derivative identity from women who are finding empowerment through self-centering. I diagram this dynamic as follows:

POWERLESS $\dfrac{\text{identity}}{\text{through}}$ →   EMPOWERED
WOMEN   WOMEN

This dynamic is not easily recognized among women because seeking identity derivatively has been and is the norm for self-actualization and personal power for women. The only difference in this dynamic is that women are seeking it through other women who are seen as powerful, instead of through powerful men. Transactions among women in this kind of dynamic can become stressful. There seems to develop an approach-withdrawal situation that is in constant need of maintenance, and a great deal of energy is required to keep lines of communication open. Because what is happening is not always recognized, issues in this kind of relationship are not always honestly dealt with. The dynamic may be further complicated if the women involved buy into the male definition of power as competition. Often women will attempt to compete with men by competing hard with each other along the partriarchal power model. In such a system competing against each other seems at least to give women a chance to experience some semblance of power. However, we hurt ourselves when we uncritically use this power system against each other, consciously or unconsciously. In relationships where women seek to gain self-power through other empowered women, close affiliation ties often are abandoned out of sheer exhaustion on both sides.

Moving away from the dynamic of identity power traps for women and men, I experience in part and envision fully two corrective dynamics in the journey toward embodiment, empowerment, and androgyny as the church's presence in the world. The first dynamic involves men who are rejecting the dehumanizing use of patriarchal power and seeking their own embodied empowerment as androgynous males. These men connect with women who are learning to value their body-selves and finding, through affiliation with other women and through their own centered identities, their capacity to be autonomous, assertive, rational selves. No one "gets" power from anyone except as a mutual flow of empowering presence. I illustrate this dynamic as follows:

$$\text{EMPOWERED} \quad \xleftrightarrow[\substack{\text{reciprocal} \\ \text{interchange}}]{\text{identity}} \quad \text{EMPOWERED}$$
$$\text{WOMEN} \qquad\qquad\qquad\qquad \text{MEN}$$

To develop my individual presence within my present position, I need several important tools. The first is *time*. I find it vital to take the time to experience, reflect, and integrate myself in situations of ministry in a different way than I experience, Vic, my co-worker, and other colleagues with whom I work. The people that our pastoral team serves in church and community also need time to experience the differences and similarities between us and to integrate them.

In developing unique identity and leadership, the second tool I need is psychological *space* to risk within my position. This is necessary for women in female-male teams, especially at this point in time, because more than likely the male team member is older or at least has more experience than his female counterpart. Women can experience two dangers here. They either can adapt and develop a derivative identity in leadership style which denies their own presence, or they can struggle to carve out their own presence—sometimes at great odds. Women confront the patriarchal power of the male norm for presence and leadership, running the risk of threatening male leadership and authority, and in some cases even a man's concept of his masculinity. This is true anywhere the female pastor attempts to develop her own leadership style, whether it is within the congregation, in synodical relationships, or within a female-male team. These factors, however, all are dependent on the woman pastor and the particular man she is relating to. In reciprocal, empowered relationships between women and men, these dangers often are diminished to manageable degrees.

Besides the time and space provided for me in my dual team calling, I also need the tool of *support*. This is important in a variety of areas. First, it is vital that my co-worker and I have a mutual respect for our individual leadership styles, where they are different and where they are similar. In work relationships this is not always as simple as it sounds. *Both* Vic and I are responsible for allowing the reciprocity between us to flow, although the task may be different for him than for me. For example, I need to discover my own autonomy as unique, female presence in leadership. Regardless of how supportive Vic is, he cannot do that for me. As I take responsibility to develop my own presence, however, his support of my uniqueness is important to us as a team and for the image our co-pastorate presents to the congregation, community, and synod. Moreover, the just and reciprocal relationship between us calls for the discovery and development of his own embodied and androgynous presence. That is his responsibility in an equalitarian female-male team relationship. My support of him in his own integration is my contribution to the process and the team relationship.

This delicate balance of awareness between autonomous development of identity and leadership among women and men who work together is a vital link in equalitarian team ministry. If the balance is lost, the male norm will dominate the relationship in both obvious and subtle ways. For instance, women tend to view success in leadership as affiliation through expressive presence, and men tend to view successful leadership as instrumental goal setting and task orientation. As female and male teams seek to develop androgynous styles of leadership, where expressive and instrumental styles are valued and used, women need to be continually aware of the danger of falling into derivative male identity, and men need to be continually conscious of their tendency to buy into patriarchal power systems and disembodied identity.

To create a space for women to reflect and develop their own leadership, Lutheran Metropolitan Ministries sponsors a local professional women's support group. This group is made up of women who work at a variety of professions in the city, and the focus of the discussions ranges from learning to value unique female experience to understanding and dealing with female-male working relationships on the job. Included are women who deal on a day-to-day basis with big company politics in performance appraisals, job promotions, and pay raises.

The secular world, however, does not have the corner on expressions of patriarchal power. Church polity also is in need of programs to aid women and men in perceiving and changing the abuses of power. One small, struggling committee of the Nebraska Synod of which I am a part specifically attempts to raise these issues. The Committee on Wholeness for Women and Men is made up of a core group who are concerned for justice and wholeness for the sexes in church, ministry, and society. In recent years the committee has weathered a variety of storms but now has managed to gain some presence in the synod. One of our recent tasks was to develop a workshop for congregations, church councils, standing committees, and pastoral call committees who choose to consider calling a woman candidate. This workshop will deal with the dynamics of women and men working together in church, ministry, and society.

Another reason the equalitarian balance in female-male teams is vital is that potent women believe they are powerless because they accept the definition of power as instrumental and not expressive. In leadership they tend to prove themselves by instrumental rather than by expressive standards. Women waste time when they buy into the efficiency, statistical standards of success. There is a reason why lay women in congregations, even though they are in the majority, often find it difficult to assume provocative leadership outside their traditional roles and relegated areas. There is a reason why I, as a woman pastor, share with some lay women their feelings of powerlessness in church structures that almost exclusively reflect male models of leadership, presence, authority, and decision making. Invisibility is a state of nonbeing. As women, we will not know our unique potency until we begin to see and experience its effect and change on the male reality all around us.

My dual team position also provides the equalitarian reciprocity between female and male in an authentic co-pastorate. The co-pastorate model, which embodies the justice relationship issues of empowerment and androgyny, challenges the patriarchal power model of senior pastor and associate or assistant for both women and men. Just and whole relationships among women and men in leadership cannot be actualized on a model of hierarchical power. Autonomous identity and unique leadership formation for women who participate in such a model with a male is seriously truncated. The challenge of the church itself, and for its presence in society as an institution of justice, is to commit itself to the development of equalitarian leadership styles. I add here that men suffer also under this power structure in full development of their identity and leadership. In my present position as co-pastor with Vic at Augustana, responsibilities are split as equally as possible between us. We try to honor our different interests and talents in our choices, and the leadership provided in the particular areas we claim is respected between us. In embodying this reciprocal relationship to the congregation, sometimes Vic has to help the congregation and others in the synod to disengage him as the main authority figure and to perceive him as an equal team member with me. We both are careful, however, to permit people their choices in pastoral leadership for funerals, weddings, baptisms, and pastoral counseling.

As co-directors of Metropolitan Ministries, our equalitarian perspective is less distinct than at Augustana. Vic founded the agency ten years ago. His community and interchurch connections are well established. Yet here, too, while I serve the ministries already established, I am responsible for developing my own programs. Often the justice issues Vic and I undertake are different; others we work on together. At Augustana and at Lutheran Metropolitan Ministries the model of the co-pastorate we strive for involves the equalitarian division of labor and tasks (instrumental leadership) and presence (expressive leadership) as each of us develops our unique leadership style.

The other corrective dynamic that I experience in part and envision fully in the journey to embodiment, empowerment, and androgyny is the authentic affiliation between women and women. I illustrate this dynamic as follows:

EMPOWERED WOMEN ←——— identity ———→ EMPOWERED WOMEN
reciprocal interchange

As women begin to relate together as identities separate from men and become centered within themselves as individuals, they can begin to use the attributes they've learned as body-selves (such as nurturing, centering, sacrificial giving in reciprocal relationship) with each other as they've done with men. The challenge for women in establishing their own whole, just relationships with one another is to begin to embody the unique empowerment of each woman as self. The woman who seeks personal power needs to realize that what she experiences in the empowered woman is what already is present in herself. The presence empowered women find in mutual interchange with other empowered women is themselves, empowered.

As my calling affords me time to integrate, space to risk my uniqueness, and support through reciprocal interchange with my male counterpart, I also need the opportunity of *affiliation* with other women as a vital component in my ministry. In developing my unique leadership as a woman and pastor, I need the empowerment of other female presence. For many women clergy at this point other ordained female colleagues are hard to come by. In such a case I find strong affiliation with empowered lay women inside and outside the church who are dealing with similar development of leadership and identity. The staff position at Lutheran Metropolitan Ministries also affords me the opportunity to produce programs, activities, and conferences for women that provide the vital affiliation among us. This comradery among women is important for two reasons. First, while comradeship is possible and desirable with male colleagues, often it is difficult to break through the "old boys club" rules and belong to the group without giving up some of who we are as women. Elizabeth Bettenhausen has commented on this phenomenon: "Women can move closer to male kinds of power, but they have to sacrifice some traditional femininity. If women play the power game economically, politically, religiously in the system and keep their sexuality as they've expressed it traditionally, it is unacceptable. Often times women have to give up their biological [body-selves] parts if they're going to play in the system's rules and assume leadership roles."[12] Second, professional women especially need to affiliate with each other because it is easy to become entrapped into valuing a linear (male) model of reality and leadership as opposed to a cyclical or circular (female) model.[13]

In a summary of these two corrective dynamics in relationship, one characteristic stands out. Identity formation in these dynamics is not derivative. The models are equalitarian and value the unique empowerment of each human presence in the interchange of relationship. Just and holistic relating is the payoff in these dynamics. The implication for the church's social ministry is implicit here. As Christian women and men model whole and just relationships, the church's identity to the world as embodied, empowered androgynous presence is deepened and enriched. When the church reflects justice by embodying it within its own institutions, it empowers other institutions and peoples. The empowered aspect of embodied justice in the church itself is the concrete relationships it is able to establish within the world. This perspective allows the church more opportunity "to be" with the world in reciprocal interchange and to exercise a more expressive style of leadership, which is a vital component in creating just relationships. In this reciprocity the church sows the seeds of change in situations of social injustice. The perspective of embodied, androgynous presence as an element of social change implies a marriage of expressive and instrumental styles of leadership within the church. This union of "being" and "doing" leadership styles is becoming more and more visible as women are participating more fully as clergy and lay leaders within church, ministry, and society. I experience a holistic, rounding out of angular, linear models of leadership with the fuller presence of women in the church. This phenomenon will need to be observed continually and documented by women and men who work together if the justice issues intrinsic in the meshing of the two models are to be embodied.

My dual position affords me the opportunity to develop an expressive style of leadership that leans heavily on personal presence. In the expressive presence I offer, people who are curious, afraid, or hostile to the ordination of women can come close to me and "be" with me as a person. As they encounter a woman as pastor, they find it more difficult to talk about the concept of ordaining women without acknowledging the real human person they have experienced. Being present to people as a pastor who is female has an important influence on raising their consciousness. It is important for ordained women and other women in society to value their embodied presence as female. In team relationships with men it is especially important to take opportunities to develop leadership autonomously yet in tandem with male counterparts.

To say our movement toward an embodied, androgynous, empowered professional leadership at Lutheran Metropolitan Ministries and Augustana has been effortless would be grossly inaccurate. To say that we have succeeded completely in embodying wholeness and justice as equal partners in our relationship with each other and with the people we serve in the congregation and through social ministry at Metropolitan Ministries is equally inaccurate. The process has been filled with struggle and pain as well as real joy. To embody justice, whether in church or society, always is a process in continual need of dynamic evaluation. It involves becoming embodied, androgynous, empowered servants and prophets. These "becoming" relationships among women and men will bring out the most positive and negative aspects in human development and change. For women and men to change what at times seem to be intrinsic patterns of relating to one another will not happen overnight. But it will not happen at all unless both invest equally in planned change. This investment among women and men who work together must always be made on a professional level as well as a personal gut level. I won't pretend it's an easy journey. Yet for those of us in the church who believe in the integrity of the embodied gospel in issues of social justice, I ask, do we have an alternative route?

The eventual justice goal for ordained women is for equal integration with men in the whole fabric of church and ministry. However, if the church recognizes the profound depth of the justice issue involved for women and men in our society, intentional affirmative action (such as exhibited in the call I presently hold) is a vital and necessary component for change now and in the future. Sexism still is to be recognized fully by the church as a serious malady. Patriarchal power and hierarchy still dominate the structural reality of the church. Disembodied presence still is the superior norm for human identity for the church. To believe these intrinsic conditions can change without wholehearted investment, painful self-reflection, intentional affirmative action, and much binding up of past and present wounds would be the cruelest of injustices. My vision is that the church must continue to invest in justice by reflecting on its own actions or inactions and providing intentional opportunities for women within its own structure. Further, I believe the church needs to challenge itself continually by recognizing and documenting to society the changes women already are bringing to the structures of the church. The church must lead the celebration of the ways women are increasing the quality of life in personal relationships and institutions.

The challenge to the church's social ministry to be embodied, empowered, androgynous presence to itself and in society is both joyful and painful. It requires integrity and honesty. It is the church's mission in the world as the incarnate presence of Jesus Christ.

Notes

1. Al Frisbe, "No Happy Ending . . . Alien's Dream Proves Impossible," Omaha *World-Herald*, Aug. 16, 1978.

2. James B. Nelson, *Embodiment: An Approach to Sexuality and Christian Theology* (Minneapolis: Augsburg Publishing House, 1978), p. 13.

3. Ibid., p. 39.

4. Ibid., p. 18.

5. James McKenna, "The Private 'I': A Guide for Winners," unpublished manuscript, pp. 151-52.

6. Sheila Collins, *A Different Heaven and Earth* (Valley Forge, Penn.: Judson Press. 1974), p. 51.

7. Nelson, *Embodiment*, pp. 261-63.

8. Nelson, *Embodiment*, p. 58.

9. Cited in Robert Bellah, *The Broken Covenant: American Civil Religion in Time of Trial* (New York: Seabury Press, 1975), pp. 105-6.

10. Nelson, *Embodiment*, pp. 268-70.

11. Eleanor Haney, "God and Wo/man: A Feminist Perspective," *Dialog*, Summer 1977, pp. 182-83.

12. Elizabeth Bettenhausen, "Does Power Have Gender?," lecture delivered at Women's Leadership Conference, sponsored by Lutheran Metropolitan Ministries, Omaha, Nebraska, 1977.

13. Ibid.

THE
TASK
OF
ENABLING

Blanqui Otaño-Rivera

It is never easy to be the first to do anything. I keep reminding myself of this whenever I find the going rough as the first woman minister in the United Presbyterian Church in Puerto Rico.

I was the first in my family to break away from the Catholic Church. When I was nine years old and getting ready to make my first communion, I refused to confess to a priest, left the church, and never returned. Two years later I was invited to visit a United Presbyterian Church. I joined with

The Rev. Blanqui Otaño-Rivera is pastor of Hugh O'Neill Memorial United Presbyterian Church in San Juan, Puerto Rico. A graduate of the University of Puerto Rico with a major in business administration, she received her M.Th. from the Latin America Biblical Seminary in Costa Rica. After completing seminary, she was employed for a time by the women's program unit of the United Presbyterian Church. She then served a church in Guánica, Puerto Rico, prior to assuming her present position.

enthusiasm because I could understand what they were talking about. The service was in Spanish, not Latin; but even more to the point, it pertained to my everyday life. After that, my life was like that of any other young person in my community—school during the week and church on Sunday.

When I graduated from the University of Puerto Rico, I was unhappy because I knew I wanted to do something meaningful with my life, but I didn't know what. At that time I was very much involved with my local church. I prayed to God to help me have a clear understanding of what I really wanted to do. Gradually it became clear that I wanted to work in the church. I listened to stories of women missionaries and was convinced that my call was to be a missionary in Latin America. I decided to attend the Latin America Biblical Seminary in San José, Costa Rica. My parents did not want me to go so far away, and my local church supporters wanted me to go to a seminary in the United States. But I was determined to go to Costa Rica, and in time they supported my decision.

While I was in seminary, I began to feel that my call was to work in my own country. After three wonderful years in Costa Rica, I returned home and joined the staff of the United Presbyterian Church in Caparra Terrace, San Juan. I was called a missionary, but the job was more like that of an assistant pastor. During this time, while reading literature from our denomination in the United States, I discovered that the United Presbyterian Church ordains women ministers. I was excited about the possibility and began to pray for assurance of a call to the ministry. Eventually I heard the call loud and clear, but my family and friends were not sympathetic. That was the first of many obstacles that lay ahead.

I became a member of the candidates committee of the Presbytery of San Juan, but I received little orientation and often had to do my own research to find the correct procedure. People kept asking me if I was sure. How did I know that God wanted women to be ministers? Men and women alike would say, "Men won't like a woman minister," and "You will never get married." In spite of the obstacles, I finished all the requirements for the ministry, including five written tests in English which were required by the United Presbyterian Church in the States.

When I was finally ready to go to a local church, I waited and waited, but no call came. There were churches on the island without pastors, but none called me. The judicatories did nothing to help place me in a church or the chaplaincy, which were the only alternatives for a minister at that time, nor could I get a job as a professor of religion at the university.

Consequently, I migrated to the United States for the same reason most Puerto Ricans migrate—to get a job. I worked for six weeks on a special program for Spanish-speaking Protestant women in New York and then joined the women's program unit of the United Presbyterian Church as a staff person for Hispanics on the East Coast and Puerto Rico.

Three-and-a-half years later, I received a call from the United Presbyterian Church in Guánica, a small town in the southwestern part of Puerto Rico. I worked there for four-teen months. Then I received a call from the Hugh O'Neill Memorial United Presbyterian Church in old San Juan, and it is this church that I now serve.

The Hugh O'Neill Memorial Church is located in a mostly commercial and tourist area of the city. It is half a block from *La Fortaleza*, the governor's residence, and across the street from the Department of State offices. The congregation is not large, but it is diverse. I particularly appreciate the opportunity to establish close relationships with the parishioners and create various programs.

My story is similar to that of many women who live in a patriarchal or *machista* society. In order to understand our brand of patriarchy, however, one must know something about our cultural, political, and religious development.

Puerto Rico, as well as other nations in Latin America, has been a victim of European and North American invasions. With all the invaders—French, Dutch, Spanish, Portuguese, and North American—there was a radically acquisitive attitude toward indigenous life and culture. When the Spaniards arrived in Puerto Rico, for instance, they took over the land, the women, and much of the culture from the native Tainos Indians.

The Tainos were an agrarian people, and they considered the land sacred. Thus the Spaniards deprived them of a vital and authentic religious expression. The Tainos were forced to accept the "superior" religion of the Spaniards, even though they did not understand this foreign religion. Eventually they acquiesed because they believed that the gods of the Spanish invaders were greater and more powerful than their own, or perhaps because they thought this was a good way to ingratiate themselves with their conquerors.

The Catholic Church rationalized, to a certain extent, the colonialization of Puerto Rico by Spain for four centuries, and during that time it helped to mold the social institutions and attitudes of the people. During the nineteenth century, church leaders discouraged young people from studying in schools of "the American democracy" because they felt it was a corrupting element of secularist thought. Today young people are discouraged from studying in Latin America so they will not come under the influence of liberation theology!

When Puerto Rico became a U.S. territory in 1898, the door was opened to Protestant influence. The Catholic hierarchy opposed this new religious "invasion," but the Protestants were protected by the United States government. The newly arrived Protestant clergy initially served the spiritual needs of the growing number of North American residents on the island. The church which I serve, for example, was founded in 1902 with thirty-eight members, all of them from the United States. Puerto Ricans became members of the church in 1904, but until 1917 the pastor was American.

The growth of the Protestant church challenged the Catholics. It seems that the Protestant work ethic was more appealing to many than the traditional religious practices of the Catholic Church. The ideal of some Protestants that material prosperity is a favorable sign from God appealed to a people who had a great admiration for the prosperity of the United States. The Puerto Rican churches found it easy to assimilate the religion and lifestyle brought by the North American missionaries. They also became completely dependent on them for human and financial resources.

Ironically, it has been American Protestant church leaders who in more recent times have made Latin Americans aware of the indignity of this assimilation and dependency. They have helped us understand our situation and have given us opportunities to develop ourselves. When the United Presbyterian Church in Mexico asked for a moratorium on missionaries and financial help from the States, the U.S. church supported the notion. The moratorium provided an opportunity for the growth of both churches.

Not all of our church leaders, however, have caught the vision. In my opinion, leadership of my denomination in Puerto Rico perpetuates the Americanization of Puerto Ricans. This is easy to understand when we still receive money, literature, and training from the United States. The United Presbyterian Church in Puerto Rico does not have its own constitution; we are one of the fifteen synods with only three presbyteries. That means we have only nine delegates in the General Assembly, our denomination's overall decision-making body, to speak for us. Some of us are members of denominational committees, but often we are described as not being active participants—descriptions that many times are true because English is a foreign language to us and because the discussion is not relevant to the realities of our people. On the other hand, often when we do present our concerns, they are not included in the agenda.

There are two types of church leaders in Puerto Rico. One is faithful to the U.S. interests but paradoxically insists that the church is not supposed to get involved in politics. These people preach and offer interpretations of Scripture translated from English which are irrelevant to our lives. The other leaders have had their consciousness raised and are seriously dealing with the contradictions we live with. Women form a significant part of this second group. They make up 68 percent of the membership of our churches and are developing strong leadership skills. They try to involve men because they believe that God calls men and women to work together, though this is hard work because some men believe liberation applies to themselves but not to women. They would allow women to work in the church but not to participate in the decision-making process.

We recognize that the oppression of women is not unique to our island. The oppression of women in the so-called developed countries, however, is very different from the oppression of women in underdeveloped countries.

A church that has developed with the contradictions I have described needs leadership development. There are three types of people in the church—those whose consciousness has been raised regarding our society; those whose membership in the church goes back several years and who largely support the status quo; and the great mass of people, who are members of the church but do not exercise any leadership. In many ways this last group offers the greatest possibilities—if they have the help of the tiny minority in the first group. They are eager to learn and grow, though sometimes they become frustrated by the authoritarian leadership of some church officials.

Many church members look to the pastor as the person who knows everything, who has all the answers. They would like to participate in that knowledge and leadership, though most of them feel incompetent. They are insecure in the church, even though many are leaders in their jobs or communities. These people have gifts and potential, abilities that can be used in the church.

It is sad to hear a person who is asked to participate in worship say, "I don't know how to pray in public," or "If I stand up, I get nervous." The people who say that often are professionals, but it is hard for some of them to imagine that their talents can be used in the church. Probably one reason is that our people think of life in two categories: the spiritual, which encompasses prayer or church activities, and the secular, which includes their job and home life. Many people simply don't make the connection between these two worlds, and the church is the loser.

Another barrier to full participation in the life of the church is sex-role stereotyping. Women are educated to be good housewives, while men are trained to be good professionals. Women develop skills related to their work at home and men to their profession or occupation. It is necessary to point out the special talents of both women and men in order to spark their interest and motivation to be more active in the church. A major part of my ministry is looking for ways to help people claim their talents and possibilities.

In our church, we divide the work into committees. Because in the past there was a tendency to have the same people on all the committees, we now look carefully to see who might work into a new role. We approach these people, explaining the requirements of the task and the reason we believe they can do a good job. We support them and provide recognition for work well done.

Another source of resistance to the participation of lay people in local church activities is the notion that the pastor is being paid to do the work and so the church is the pastor's. Just as dangerous is a similar attitude toward one member of the congregation. This creates the one-person ownership concept, where a single person feels free to make decisions and act for others. Needless to say, this presents a delicate situation for the pastor. One way of handling it is to keep emphasizing correct procedures established by the denomination so that criticism does not become a personal matter. In our church, we spend one session in the Sunday school each month on just such procedures.

Church people need to experience equality; they need to feel that they are all children of God, regardless of race, sex, education, or social standing. They need confidence and assurance from the pastor and the leaders of the judicatories.

Our local church has many older members. When I started working with them, one of the first questions they raised was, "What are you doing with so many older members if we are good for nothing?" I was amazed by the question but soon discovered these feelings of inadequacy were widespread in the congregation.

"I believe that people are good because they are children of God, regardless of sex, age, position, or gifts," was my first answer. I immediately began to deal with those feelings of low self-esteem. From that time on, I knew that a major part of my job would be building up people and supporting them.

After attitudes and feelings are dealt with, training is important. People need to develop the resources and skills they discover. These include how to lead worship, the planning process, parliamentary procedure, techniques of evangelism, and so on. I feel that the entire congregation must participate in some way in the planning process of the church, though it is not practical to have the direct participation of large numbers. We find we can include them through special questionnaires for that purpose.

In our church, the congregation is invited to bring suggestions or commentaries to church the Sunday before the session meeting that is held on Wednesday. I do not promise to do what they ask, but I do promise to give it serious consideration. Another way to gather opinions and ideas is to listen carefully when members of the church gather informally and begin talking about the program of the church. If we as pastors are sensitive enough and are able to get our people to talk, we will receive many suggestions and develop a good sense of what people like and dislike, need or do not need.

Getting people involved also takes a sensitivity to the sex or age group involved. As in most of the churches in Puerto Rico, our congregation has only a few men. This is a cultural phenomenon which we are just now beginning to study. We have had some success, and some men who were previously inactive are now becoming interested.

We have a wonderful group of children. They participate in the Sunday worship, and I take them into consideration when I am planning and giving my sermons. At communion, the children who are too young to participate in the sacrament are given a grape so they will feel a part of the community. We are looking forward to starting a Children's Day celebration in our church. Twice a year in the Sunday school I have open conversations with the children. The parents also are encouraged to talk with their children at home about the church service and give me their comments.

Right now our church is having a beautiful experience with one of the members. When I first came to the church, I was looking for people to read the Scriptures and offer prayers during Sunday worship. When I asked one woman to lead the prayer of illumination, she said no, explaining that she had never done that sort of thing and was always very nervous in front of people. I answered that I was sure she prayed at home, and I suggested she write out a prayer at home and bring it with her next week. Her immediate response was, "Can we write prayers?" I explained to her that the Holy Spirit guides us when we sit down, think, and write, as well as when we pray aloud in public.

She agreed to write a prayer, and the next Sunday she prayed in public for the first time. The prayer in her own words was full of feelings of gratitude and assurance of guidance. Later on that day, we were talking about how important it is to communicate with God in our own language, and I discovered that this woman was full of good ideas. I have kept in touch with her to offer support and encouragement through conversations at church activities and visits to her home.

Because our congregation lives scattered throughout the metropolitan area, it is very difficult to get together at night. We have Thursday evening worship in homes in different areas. Once when we were planning a worship service, this woman offered to be in charge. Two weeks before her worship service she called me to explain what she had in mind. Her theme was "God's Creation." The congregation was asked to participate in the Scripture readings. Then she read from the local newspaper to spark a group discussion on Christian responsibility in the world.

I was very impressed at her creativity and have been pleased with her increasing ease in talking about her faith in God. She has come alive through leadership development.

Some people think ministers are special people with a mystical relationship with God. When I shared my personal struggle of trying to be faithful to God's call with my congregation, I found that a new and beautiful relationship was established with the people. Even though they were not used to receiving this kind of sharing, they responded; they became conscious of the fact that sex discrimination is a reality in our church today. As a result, they are more understanding, and a deeper mutual respect has developed. We have become allies in fulfilling the mission of the church.

I understand that this style of work puts the pastor in a vulnerable position. But it is necessary to get close to the people one is trying to serve. The church today is challenged to find those alternatives which will develop leadership among the faithful. It needs men and women working together, under the guidance of God, to fulfill its mission on earth.

SHAPED BY THE SPIRIT

Susan W. N. Ruach

It took three weeks for the crisis to come to a head. I knew it was a crisis of major proportions; yet it was so quiet. Even as I look back on it now, the quietness inspires a sense of awe. Yet at the end of those three weeks I knew as surely as I have ever known anything that I could not continue to be a local church pastor unless I got more solid grounding, more depth, more in touch with God.

This crisis of faith and vocation thus began a much more intensive phase of my spiritual journey. I had been pastor in two other local churches—once as an associate and once as copastor with my husband. When the crisis occurred, I was serving in a church where I was the only pastor. In fact, the only other person being paid there was a part-time custodian whom I seldom ever saw. Perhaps part of what caused the crisis was that I couldn't turn to nearby colleagues (or anyone

---

The Rev. Susan W. N. Ruach is on the staff of the Conference Council on Ministries of the South Indiana Conference of the United Methodist Church. Her areas of responsibility include spiritual formation, Christian education, and ordained and diaconal ministry. Before moving to her present position she served churches in Beech Grove, Batesville, and Seelyville, Indiana. She is a graduate of Boston University School of Theology and holds the Ed.D. degree from Indiana University.

else) anymore for support and encouragement on a daily basis. At other times in my ministry, I had tried prayer, Bible study, and other devotional disciplines; but my attempts had been sporadic at best and never a very important part of my life. I *needed* a faith relationship to God in a new way.

I began reading books on prayer (a few pages a day) and trying the different kinds of prayer that I was reading about—the Jesus prayer, meditation, contemplation, and guided imagery. I tried to discipline myself to a daily time of Scripture reading, meditation, and intercessory prayer, and found the practice really hard to do every day. Some days I was too busy; some days, I forgot; and some days, I just plain didn't want to. Finally, after six months, I decided that I needed someone besides God to help me set aside and stick to a daily time of prayer.

I went to a two-day clergy continuing education event on prayer and spirituality looking for someone who would meet with me regularly and who would inquire about my prayer life. Fortunately, I found another clergywoman there who also wanted such support. We met every other week for lunch for eight months, with the agreement that somewhere in the course of conversation each would inquire of the other, "How's it going with your prayer life?"

The conversations and the accountability were very helpful—so much so that when the changing circumstances of our lives caused us to stop meeting, I looked for and found a spiritual director with whom I met for three-and-a-half years. We usually met every two weeks for about an hour. She gave me encouragement, gentle stability, balance, reassurance, direction and vision. Knowing I would be talking to her, I began to reflect on what was going on in my life and where I saw God acting. During our appointment, she often gave me the right book or said the word I needed to hear. She always attributed her ability to give such help to the Holy Spirit.

I also began to try some of the classical disciplines of the Christian faith—fasting, study, silence, meditation, various forms of prayer, solitude, reading the Bible for the word in it that God was speaking to me, devotional reading, and keeping a spiritual diary. I began to feel a new sense of balance and wholeness. And I began to see the spiritual in places I had been unwilling to look before.

Those months were times of great excitement and exuberance, but I also struggled to look at myself under the gentle guidance of the Spirit. As I would reflect on what I had said or done and on my motives, I saw things I didn't like about myself and recognized feelings of loneliness, jealousy, greed, and insecurity that I had refused to acknowledge before. Seeing the ugliness in me and having periods where God seemed absent and I felt dry made these some of the hardest days of my life. During these days I cried, prayed, wrote, talked to friends, and in the midst of it all was given grace and growth.

Through reflection on my actions and motives, I began to understand myself better, and to be more willing to look at what was going on inside of me. I gradually became more sensitive to my own body as well as to my emotions. There began to be a new openness to my own feelings of pain, sexual arousal, sadness, fatigue, joy, peace, and so on, because I had less need to hide them from myself and others. As I became more open to myself, I found myself more willing to listen to others, to understand where they were and what was going on in their lives. New thoughts or ideas, a book I needed to read, an old or new friend seemed to come to me at times when I needed them most; such gifts I attribute to God's care.

I discovered that there was a classical name for what was happening: spiritual formation. I like to define it as a process by which one allows God's Spirit to transform one's self into a person of Christ-like spirit. Spiritual formation involves growing in one's relationship to God and one's relationship to other people and all of creation. Even our way of living in and our responses to the systems and institutions of our day are involved in spiritual formation. As we become more like Christ, our trust in God grows, our need to be in control lessens, and we become increasingly clearer channels through which God's gentle and tough love flows. We become both more compassionate and less willing to put up with injustice in any form.

While the term "spiritual formation" may be new, especially to Protestants, the process itself is not new. In Protestantism we have more likely called it "growing in one's faith," "our spiritual journey," "the devotional life," "the inner journey," or some such phrase. Our understanding of spiritual formation has often included only the specific time of Bible study and intercessory or confessional prayer. We need to see again that spiritual formation or growing in our faith touches our whole life. Our spirituality is far more than just the way we pray or what we pray in some narrow sense; it is how we live all of our lives, the totality of our response to God.

I have also learned that each person is unique, and therefore each person's path to God is different. I believe that we must respect every person's path, trusting that even as God wants me to grow and is helping me to grow, God is working with each person and helping each person to grow too. Therefore my responsibility is to share my path with others, inviting them to take from my path what they find helpful and to leave the rest.

Spiritual formation is not something we have to insist others must do—another activity added to a busy schedule. The desire for God is already in each of us. Coming from within, it needs only to be awakened, encouraged, coaxed out, and then enjoyed. Often our spirituality is nourished in the most unexpected ways, especially as God works through the ordinariness of our days and in the things that we take most for granted. A part of the process is developing eyes that truly see.

Prayer, as awareness of God, is therefore crucial. I like to think of prayer as "getting ourselves into God's force field." To pray is to live in the presence of God, and it is in prayer that we experience deeply and consistently the undeserved, relentless love of God for us in spite of everything else.

As my own times of prayer and connection to God became more important to me, I began to want the congregation that I was serving to find an increase of God in their lives too. I began by simply talking to people, sharing in conversations what was happening to me. Soon our congregation decided to emphasize prayer during one Lenten period. Part of this emphasis was to be a six-sermon series on prayer. When I shared these plans with a pastor friend, he told me, "I tried to preach a four-sermon series once on prayer and ran out of material after the second one." I was intimidated by that remark for three days, but in a burst of confidence I decided that maybe I knew more about prayer than he did. The six areas I covered were the importance of prayer, how one learns to pray, hindrances to prayer, prayer as asking, prayer as confession, prayer as listening (and were I to do it again, I would put in prayer and action). Although there were difficult moments in the sermon series, lack of material was not one of them!

In addition to the six sermons, we also had a program of prayer partners. Everyone who wanted to participate wrote his or her name on a piece of paper and put it in an offering plate. Then we passed the offering plate around and those who had put their names in took someone else's name out. The people who participated in this program seemed to find it meaningful, especially in the growth in relationship between the partners and in being prayed for. The Lenten emphasis also included two groups doing a study on prayer using Maxie Dunham's *Workbook on Living Prayer*,[1] as well as a weekend workshop on prayer to help us learn how to pray better.

I found that many people in the congregation (as well as other pastors) were interested in growing in their faith and in the ability to live more Christian lives, and were also interested in prayer. I discovered these people in meetings, informal conversations, chance remarks, over cups of tea in homes, through something that was said or shared. Several of these people had lots of questions. Congregational leaders and I tried to create an atmosphere where *any* question was acceptable by taking such questions or thoughts seriously and by sharing some of our questions and struggles.

As ideas would come, they would be discussed; frequently we put them into practice. For instance, we used prayer and learning to pray as a part of the children's time in worship by asking them to pray for a sick person they all knew, imagining that the person was healthy again. And we talked about needing to learn how to pray just as one learns how to skip or hop. We also instituted a period of silence in the worship service following corporate confession, and had a weekend retreat on spiritual renewal. We set up a program in which each week certain families were designated as "prayer families." We prayed for three or four families each week, and within each year's time we had prayed for every family in the church.

Richard Foster's *Celebration of Discipline*,[2] which tells how to practice several traditional disciplines of the Christian life was so helpful to me that I bought a second copy and gave it to the lay leader of the church who I thought would also find it helpful. A couple of months later she came back to me and said, "I've been reading that book you gave me. I need to talk about it." Not too long after that at a Council on Ministries meeting, she suggested that we have a study on *Celebration of Discipline*, which we did.

I had begun the discipline of fasting, which is abstaining from food for spiritual reasons such as growing closer to God, as a sign of repentance, or while seeking guidance from God. I began because I hoped it would help me grow closer to God. I also extended it beyond fasting from food to fasting for one year from taking on any new responsibilities that I was not already committed to. I also fasted from time to time from buying any new clothes. (Most recently I fasted from hurrying during the period of Lent.) It never occurred to me that anyone else in the church would be interested. But a few people began to mention fasting to me, either asking questions about it or making references to their own practice of fasting. I began to feel like it was time for a sermon on fasting. Out of that and the sermons on prayer came sermons on some of the other disciplines—Bible study, reflection, simplicity, and confession.

Out of those early struggles emerged ways to think more systematically about designing programs for, and creating an atmosphere that valued spiritual formation in the life of the local congregation. There are at least four areas in which work can be done in most congregations (or for that matter, on boards, agencies, committees, judicatories, or other groups) to foster spirituality.

First of all there must be *permission* given and *expectations* set. Those in leadership positions must make sure people know that having a prayer life doesn't make one "too pious." People must also know that they are in fact expected to grow in their faith, to learn how to pray, to work at the disciplines by which we become more Christ-like. Permission-giving and expectation-setting is done explicitly. It can also be shown in little ways, such as what one says about one's own life, what one teaches, what one says about prayer (and even in talking about prayer at all), in offering to pray with others, in talking about one's own struggles and times of solitude, and so on. Encouragement to grow spiritually can be given through the design of Confirmation classes, in what new members are taught, the sermons that are preached, and the kinds of programs that are offered.

The second category involves *models and examples*. While talking about ways of spiritual formation is important, often we are more encouraged to "keep at it" by watching and learning from what those around us do. The time of silence at the beginning of a meeting to help people focus on God and the purpose of the meeting can be a good example of the importance of silence in one's life. The sharing of struggles by a person who is mature in the faith can model for others that such struggles are normal. Someone who gives away possessions or volunteers a day a week in a soup kitchen out of his or her own faith commitment models the connection of the inner and outer journey. A local church may need to have examples of courageous faith lifted up to it from newsletters, sermons, and other places.

The third category is *resources*. Since people are so different, both in their personalities and their paths to God, it is important that there be a variety of resources available. Resources can be of many kinds—books, articles, tapes, workshops, retreats, classes, a place, time apart, and people, to name but a few. Obviously, no church can provide all the resources needed for every person in the congregation. However, it does seem important that each church make available a solid and healthy variety of resources, or at least give concrete recommendations and directions for getting them. This category includes communicating about what resources are available in other places as well. One church may have books to sell, while another might have a series of cassettes traded around among members. The Bible is a primary resource, through which God speaks to us both as individuals and as communities. Most churches will benefit from offering some sort of training in how one can read the Bible in such a way as to hear God speaking. This is the kind of Bible study I call "Bible pondering," in which one tries to incorporate God's Word into one's own life and soul through thoughtful reflection and repetition. Other important resources for spiritual growth are the sacraments and physical things such as crosses, icons, and pictures which communicate God's love to us in concrete ways and call us back to faithfulness.

The fourth category is *programs*. Programs devoted to spiritual formation can take many forms: an overnight retreat, a day apart once a month, a book review in the church newsletter, a study on prayer or other aspects of the journey, working in a transient center or a food kitchen on a regular basis, and so on.

In addition, there are three areas in which a congregation might explore each of the above four categories. First, there is the *life together* of the congregation—its worship, meetings, church school, and programs. A local church could monitor what permissions and expectations for spiritual development are found in worship and in church school, for instance. It could ask about the models and examples of its meetings and programs; about what resources are available for the members as they relate to each other; and about what kinds of programming would help form its life together in more Christ-like ways.

The second area of focus is on the *personal lives* of the members. Here again a local church can look at what is needed in each of the four categories. For instance, a church might ask if its members give themselves permission to spend time in prayer. Members of the church might recommend someone who could serve as a spiritual model, such as Dorothy Day, Thomas Kelly, or someone in the local community. Does the church direct its members to resources for faith development? What programs encourage personal faith growth?

The third area involves the *intersections* of the lives of the members with others in the community. What permissions and expectations about spiritual formation might members give to those in the surrounding community? What models and examples should the members and local church be setting? What resources should the life together of the congregation and the lives of the members be providing for those who are not a part of the church? Are there programs that the church ought to be providing for those outside of the church?

These categories can be combined to form a grid that can be used to think about spiritual formation in the life of a congregation in an organized way.

	Permission and Expectations	Models and Examples	Resources	Programs
Life Together				
Personal Lives				
Intersections				

To use this grid, a congregation may list in each box the ways it addresses each of the four categories across the top in relation to each of the three listed vertically. To begin, a church might list in the Life Together/Permission and Expectations box the use of silence at the beginning of meetings and in worship, and the affirmation to new members of the need to pray. Then in turn each of the other boxes may be filled out. The congregation can then see specific areas where little or nothing is being done and can choose things to do.

This grid came out of my struggle to find some systematic way of looking at spiritual formation in a group setting. Out of this process I also became aware of areas of spirituality of

particular interest to women and for which they expressed a
need. Although I have separated the areas for the discussion,
they actually flow together and interrelate in varying degrees.

Wholeness is such an area. We need to use both sides of the
brain. Body, spirit, emotions, intellect are not separate or
compartmentalized, but are all necessary in one's faith and
faith journey. We are not a series of roles—worker, spouse,
parent, child, minister, lay person, volunteer, breadwinner,
gardener, homemaker, worshipper. Rather, we are whole
people; the various responsibilities of our lives must flow
together with harmony and balance. If one part of our lives is
out of balance, it effects the other parts also. This wholeness
or sense of balance carries over to our total lifestyle, how we
use our time, energy, money, and so on. Wholeness includes
good stewardship of personal, cultural, and natural resources
as well.

Along with wholeness goes the *affirmation of the body and
body-wisdom*. The Christian church in particular has often
negated the body, and especially sexuality. When we are
more in touch with the cycles and rhythms of our bodies, we
are more open to hearing the wisdom the body has to offer
and to see the importance of nutrition and exercise in spirituality. We are not disembodied spirits, we are embodied
people. Our bodies are a part of God's good gift to us. (And if
you don't believe that there is a strong connection between
spirituality and body, just try praying in an uncomfortable
position and see how long you can last. Or consider how
hard it is to pray when you are ill.)

Part of the body's wisdom is that we cannot do everything.
We are not sufficient in ourselves; we must be willing to say
that we *need help*. As long as we think we are sufficient to run
the world or even our own lives by ourselves, we have no
need of God (Matt. 9:12). Often the discovery that we need
that which is greater than we moves us into an intensive
phase of our spiritual journey. It is the same *sense of neediness*
that enables us to support and be supported by others, to
receive guidance, and to share. And it is because some of our
needs are met that we want to help others in acts of kindness
and in fighting injustice.

Finally we need to be *more open* to explore nontraditional formulations and paths, to look at many images of God, at forms of prayer beyond only the discursive, to be more willing to experiment, more open to new possibilities. Growing in our relationship to God is more important than upholding forms or traditions for their own sake and defending what doesn't feed us.

Looking back over the last six years, the more intensive phase of my journey, I can see ways I've grown and things I've learned. I am more sensitive to my own pains and joys and I understand others' feelings better. I am able to hear with more depth. I know that spirituality can not be forced and I have even learned some ways to help willing people grow. As a congregation we have learned how to encourage people, to provide information about prayer, about the importance of an atmosphere of acceptance and that we must do things on God's time. I have discovered how social consciousness and fighting injustices come together with the inner journey, the importance of exercise and health, how to encourage others without pushing, and the joys and struggles of keeping the disciplines over the long haul. As I moved from being a parish pastor to being a conference staffer, the transitions helped me see again how easy it is to lose one's peace and become scattered over many concerns. I know anew the ease with which the disciplines of Scripture study and prayer can slip away and what happens to me when they do. As I have grown in one area, another has presented itself to work on. In some ways the journey feels a little more settled now; in other ways, almost as new as it did six years ago. In any event, one thing is certain: my journey continues and it is far from over. Indeed, those on the journey travel on by faith to the destination that is God.

Notes

1. Maxie Dunham, *Workbook on Living Prayer* (Nashville: The Upper Room, 1977).

2. Richard Foster, *Celebration of Discipline* (San Francisco: Harper & Row, 1978).

MINISTRY IN HEALING AND HEALTH CARE

Eugenia Lee Hancock

September 13, 1975. I awakened with a searing pain in my right shoulder. A foggy thought began to dawn in my brain: my rheumatoid arthritis has come back.

Several years before, while still in college, strange and seemingly unrelated symptoms had emerged in my body. Tests finally led to the diagnosis of rheumatoid arthritis. Although arthritis had pained and twisted many a relative, this particular form of crippling had not attacked anyone else in my family before.

The medical plan was simple, but not without consequence: "Twelve aspirins a day for the rest of your life." Being a cooperative patient, I began this regimen only to encounter chronic stomach problems and diarrhea. These I

The Rev. Eugenia Lee Hancock is the associate minister of Judson Memorial Church in New York City. She served as the program associate for the Women in Ministry Project of the National Council of Churches; and from 1978–81 she was assistant minister and minister for healing and health care at Central Presbyterian Church of New York City. Ms. Hancock is a graduate of Mary Baldwin College and holds the M.Div. degree from Union Theological Seminary in New York City.

endured until I departed from the hills of Virginia, where I had been an undergraduate, and moved north to seminary. Once in a new environment, my symptoms seemed to lessen and gradually disappear until finally, one glorious sunshine-filled summer, I decided that I was "cured" and threw away my aspirin bottle. Several years later, during my final year of seminary in New York, the awakening of pain unlike any I had ever known seemed like the activation of a frightening and familiar nightmare: the disease had returned. Desperate to receive some medical attention, I suffered through that first weekend armed with aspirin and headed Monday morning to the seminary infirmary, where I received an unlimited prescription for an aspirin compound with codeine.

Days rolled by. I grew depressed and frustrated. Joints swelled and grew stiff, rebelling against my insistence that they function. Exhausted and overextended, leading the double life of both seminary employee and seminary student, I became terrified when I could no longer depend upon my body to "perform" at all cost.

At Christmastime I returned to my family home to find that my grandmother, riddled by an arthritis theoretically "less benign" than my own, was facing the amputation of a leg due to the loss of circulation that had resulted from untended arthritis. As I saw her near death, I saw her fate as my own. My toes had begun to curl under, it was becoming more difficult to walk, to sit and stand, to find any shoes that would fit.

My pain, grief, and fear were intermingled as she died on the first day of the new year. Feeling battered and defeated, I returned to New York armed with a new medication prescribed by the physician who had originally provided the diagnosis, only to discover that this medicine too caused severe side effects and offered little relief to the illness that was now on a rampage in my body. In desperation I wrote a letter to the doctor back home who had named my condition. "Help, help me please find a doctor in New York. I'm terrified. I'm becoming crippled before my very eyes."

No word came. Angry and discouraged, I had had it with traditional medicine—medicines that compounded my problems and provided no relief. In the midst of all this pain, rage, and turmoil, I decided I would have to discover my own healing for myself. "Through many dangers, toils, and snares, I have already come," sing the words of "Amazing Grace." The search for my healing had led me through many dangers, toils, and snares, and ended in the church.

All in all, the illness claimed two full years of my life before I could even think of returning to any life I would consider "normal." When I did return, I was still frail and wearing braces, and I could only work and continue my final seminary studies part-time. Out of the illness, however, grew a firm conviction that the church could no longer ignore the apostolic ministry of healing, so clearly described in the New Testament and so definitively practiced by Jesus and his disciples.

"What happened to this ministry?" I asked myself. Needing all the help I could get, I returned to my religious tradition to discover the philosophical roots of healing. The very word "healing" was problematic for me. I grew up in southern West Virginia, where faith healers were charlatans and quacks, objects of scorn and contempt, who were perceived as preying upon the desperate poor. And up in the hollow, mountain folk practiced "snake handlin" as a ritual testimony to their beliefs. Healing had a magical quality, spurned by the straight and narrow standards of southern Presbyterianism.

But once faced with illness, the word "healing" gathered new meaning. I was involved in a special process, the movement from brokenness and debilitation to a state of wholeness, and "healing" best described the activity I was pursuing. My disillusionment with both the medical establishment and healers who could work "miracles" had turned me off to the notion of seeking a cure; for "cure" implied something immediate and drastic, an instantaneous elimination of symptoms.

I had been introduced to various alternative health care practices one summer at Esalen Institute in California. These had included esoteric forms of psychotherapy or "body work," which gave psychological meaning to physical symptoms. Feminism, too, had raised the important issue of self-care and taking responsibility for one's health. As I began to investigate alternatives to the orthodox approaches to "getting well," I discovered my need for a philosophy of healing, a theoretical approach to health that would put the spiritual, emotional, psychological, and existential aspects of my life into a framework. Eastern philosophies and nontraditional approaches to health care offered far more philosophically than the orthodox approach to medical care. Since modern medicine is generally based upon a mechanistic world view, there was not much room for reflection upon the theory of healing. As a patient I was instructed to put my trust in the practitioner, follow "his" orders, and abide by the authoritative prescription for a medical plan and treatment. I discovered within my self a great yearning for a theology, a philosophy to interpret, that would enable me to understand what constituted this event and the process of getting well. I wanted to know what I could do and how I could be a participant, even a partner in my own healing.

In addition to my philosophical search, I began experimenting with a smorgasbord of alternative therapies. Homeopathy, nutritional counseling, even "astral biochemistry"—nutrition by the stars. Bioenergetics, a form of psychotherapy. Massage. Hydrotherapy. Some approaches helped, others did not. I read everything about rheumatoid arthritis I could get my hands on. And I visited every practitioner who offered some hope, some end to the pain. Still I grew weaker, more crippled, no longer able to tolerate the weight of a sheet on my body, or put on socks, or lift a cup to drink. The inflammation raged on. All the while I was surrounded by loving people who would stay the night with me in my terror, brush my hair, fix my meals.

I descended into the dark night of my soul. Spiritually and theologically, I wrestled with the profound issues of illness and suffering: "Why me? Why was I suffering? Why was this happening to me?" I turned to the Book of Job and allowed myself to identify with his rage, his incredulity. That gave me strength. I was approached by more than one person who equated my religious vocation with my experience of suffering, assuming that somehow God's will was being born out, that I had been chosen, even elected, to "bear this burden." I was enraged at the thought that God was willing my suffering, and yet I searched my heart to uncover what crime I had committed, what sin I had indulged in that warranted such crippling physical pain. The notion of God as all powerful made no intellectual sense to me in light of such suffering in this world. I rejected the notion that God was the grand puppeteer who inflicted pain for some mysterious purpose.

I had shied away from prayer, especially the prayer of my childhood. But now, with the help of Job, I opened up. For the first time, I began to really discover prayer. I uttered the desperation I was feeling, the battered quality of my spirit. I learned to rage against God, and not hold God responsible for the pain. I began to know the power of Whitehead's words, first spoken to me by a colleague at Union, "God is the fellow sufferer who understands."

The presence of Jesus' healing stories in the Bible raised another question for me: "What happened? How did, (or didn't) the church deal with these stories?" These questions gave some direction to the intellectual dimension of my quest for healing. Aided by Morton Kelsey in *Christianity & Healing*,[1] and others, I began to learn about the neglect of Christianity of this ministry and began to question more actively this neglect in light of the healing activity of Jesus.

Two years after the first attack, in 1977, I resumed my seminary studies. Those years had been dominated by one theme: my desire for healing. I was desperate, and desperate people do desperate things. My efforts ranged from the most esoteric approaches, to an eventual hospitalization, where I discovered that the arthritis had been accompanied by hepatitis.

Angels in human form intervened at critical times, and revealed yet another way. Slowly, things improved—gradually, incrementally, through time. Determined to finish seminary and fueled by the questions wrought from my experience, I resumed my seminary studies part-time and enrolled in a parish-based program designed to focus on urban ministry. The last thing I wanted to do was to re-enter seminary—I wanted experience; I wanted to get out; I wanted to move on. I felt behind and embarrassed and out of the human race. Still weakened and debilitated, I wore braces on my arms, moved slowly, and limped. I felt raw and insecure, as if layers of my ego had been stripped away. I began to focus upon my intellectual task, "What happened to healing in the church?" At the end of the year, I produced my Master of Divinity Master's thesis on the subject.

My field placement offered to keep me on in a part-time capacity for the following academic year. It was during this time that I began to reflect upon a ministry in healing and health. My experience and need for a comprehensive source of support in my most critical time, along with the neglect of the healing ministry by more mainline churches, prompted me to design a proposal for an experimental ministry in healing and health care.

Writing the grant proposal helped me crystallize some of the learning from my own experience. The rationale for the ministry focused upon the crisis in health care, as well as the apostolic ministry of healing that had been "lost" in mainline churches. The problem seemed clear:

> The reformed tradition has relegated healing and health care to the domain of health care institutions, by allowing healing to be identified exclusively with the charismatic movement. No longer can we ignore our collective needs for preventive medicine, healthy lifestyle, humane and inexpensive health care, and healing. Healing must be salvaged as a ministry of the Church.[2]

Underlying the problem were several assumptions concerning healing and health care:
- that we suffer from a radical mind-body split
- that our culture indulges in an uncritical acceptance of professionals—i.e., doctors whom we expect to "fix our bodies for us"—instead of teaching us to care for ourselves
- that we are alienated from our bodies, perceiving them less as the "temple of the Holy Spirit," and more as machines to be repaired when they break down; we are unfamiliar with our bodies and their innate possibilities for healing
- that our approach to health care is oriented toward cure and not prevention; furthermore, we are uninformed about alternatives to traditional Western medicine

• that technology increasingly produces iatrogenic diseases

• that the obsolescence of the family doctor and the development of the medical complex devoted to research has eliminated the "human element"

that the approach to healing in the medical establishment is scientific, linear, and causal, and does not take into account the emotional, spiritual, ambiguous, psychic, and "human" elements.

The local congregation seemed to me a suitable and appropriate environment for a ministry in healing and health care because of its potential as a therapeutic community, opportunities for education both in terms of self-care and medical issues, and absence of competing aims that divert the medical complex from the task of healing.

Both Central Presbyterian Church in Manhattan and the Program Agency of the United Presbyterian Church in the U.S.A. agreed to jointly fund a three-year experimental ministry in healing and health care. I began that effort in the fall of 1979, supported by a group of lay persons at Central Church who formed a task force on healing and health care. Among its members were medical professionals, educators, and interested lay persons. We began to hammer out a three-pronged program that focused on three goals of the parish: worship, education, and outreach.

The first program implemented was worship. We held healing services, recognizing the complexity and variety of responses that would ensue, particularly in light of the absence of precedents for such a service in the Presbyterian tradition. We designed a simple, reformed liturgy, which emphasized both confession and the "Word." The Word offered weekly focused on some aspect of healing and health care, from the pastoral and inspirational to the pragmatic and the political.

What followed was a time of intercessory prayer and laying on of hands, which I both introduced and explained. I encouraged people to participate at their own level, and invited them to stay even if they were not motivated to participate in laying on of hands. I explained about the priesthood of all believers, the doctrine that characterized the theological thrust of the service. The emphasis of the service was on both Word and ritual, with theological perspective on the liturgical aspect of healing that was neither charismatic nor sacramental, but consistent with the Reformed tradition. (My teacher, Cyril Richardson, contributed an invaluable piece of scholarship when he outlined two types of healing in the earthly church—"charismatic" and "sacramental.")

All who were interested in participation came forward and stood in a circle. As we gathered together, I would inquire if anyone present was interested in giving or receiving laying on of hands, or offering or requesting prayer. A person who acknowledged this desire would move to the center of the circle. I would grasp his or her hands, and begin to pray for that individual, while the others in the circle laid their hands upon the person.

We gathered weekly, a small band of folk, to discover just what a healing service might be. Our conviction about the healing power of community grew. We witnessed no "zap" or miraculous elimination of symptoms, but we observed the shedding of many tears, tears of confession and release. We learned about the growth and strength of intimacy, forged from confession, and the sharp revelation of buried truths and denied pains and hidden burdens.

All kinds of people came to these services, people with physical, mental, and emotional wounds. Some people came and went, others came and stayed. Dealing with the unexpected also emerged as a challenge for the group. People frequently dropped by, lured by the sign on Park Avenue that read "Healing Service Inside." I remember once when an obviously psychotic young man came into the service. After the singing of the opening hymn, he blurted out loudly that the organist, with his bald head, looked like George Washington! He then stormed out, leaving us all dumbfounded!

Sometimes symptoms did subside. People talked of less pain, greater strength, clean X-rays. And yet, we were all aware of the dangers of making claims, of claiming that these services "caused" the cure. Making connections between the service and a "cure" was something we never championed. We grew to understand the simple reason we were there was because of the apostolic mandate and precedent "to heal," not from any claims or assurances that "we" could bring cure, or that God "would" heal through these means. We knew that humility and gratitude were essential to conducting this effort, which felt scary and audacious, but was something we indeed wanted to try.

Our theological rationale was clear to us. We stated in our announcement of these services:

> All of us need healing in one way or another, although some persons' need for healing is more obvious. We are a limited people of God, and our needs for healing, both personal and corporate, cannot be ignored. In response to this need, Central Presbyterian Church is initiating a liturgical experiment, the focus of which is healing.
>
> The healing hervices are intended not to achieve miraculous cures, but to bring to the context of worship the needs all of us have for healing of one kind or another. In this context, we are redefining healing as a process of movement of our selves toward a new wholeness—as a process at work in our daily life of the church, rather than relegating it entirely to the domain of health-care institutions.
>
> Through prayer and meditation, participants focus on their need for healing and desire for wholeness; through worship, we find personal energy and openness to the power of God, who created new life within and through us. Through discussions and exchanging information, we reflect on the paths and obstructions to health and wholeness. Together we laugh and cry, and share in the support that community can give. As a community, we are finding and claiming the process of healing as a reality in our lives.[3]

In addition, healing and health were emphasized during regular worship services. Our parish celebrated ACCESS (an inter-denominational liturgical celebration of those with handicapping conditions); co-opted laity Sunday so all participants spoke on healing and health care; "reformed" coffee hours along better nutritional principles; and investigated the accessibility of the sanctuary for handicapped people. All these efforts were really political in nature, as our task force struggled to gain parish visibility on the issues of healing and health care.

The ministry blossomed, and the task force tackled both education and outreach as the other foci of the ministry. We began the educational task slowly, first educating ourselves. When we grew more familiar with the issues, our courage empowered us to take our message into the whole congregation. We held educational programs on all kinds of topics: massage, the healing touch of Jesus, meditation, ritual.

We began to develop a library of books, and designated that every time a month contained a fifth Sunday, we would schedule an educational event focused upon healing and health care. By the time the program had ended we felt that educationally the program had been "mainstreamed"—in fact the Lenten educational series was on the topic of death and dying, sponsored by the task force. A spin-off of our educational thrust was a program entitled "Explorations in Spirituality," a progam sponsoring retreats based upon the myth of Asklepios, the Greek god of healing, as well as workshops on dreams and meditation.

Our thrust was experimental, our intent to raise issues of healing and health care as often and in as many forms as possible. Our mission objective included both research and program. We began to draw together interested clergy in the metropolitan area for conversation, and to discover how much and what was known about health care. With the help of a statistician, we designed and mailed a questionnaire to all ministers in the New York Presbytery. This instrument was used to assess the ministers' knowledge about and methods for responding to a variety of health issues, from abortion to violence. Data collected by this project was then compiled and interpreted by members of the task force. Many conclusions were drawn, but one broad generalization was evident—clergy were ill-informed about most health concerns, and failed to perceive these concerns as being within the perview of ministry. In particular, clergy display a serious lack of information regarding women's health issues.

Programmatic efforts in the mission emphasis were experimental in nature. In addition to research, we sponsored a class in rehabilitation movement for persons with debilitating chronic illnesses. A workshop for chronic illness education was designed. We initiated blood drives, and more "traditional" congregational efforts emphasizing health.

The major programmatic thrusts for the ministry of healing and health care were worship, education, and liturgy. However, I was nurtured in my understanding of the nature of healing and health and the dynamics of illness through the intimacy of frequent conversations with people who sought healing in all aspects of life.

I began to understand the value of my intuitions about the presence of community in the lives of those combatting illness. The presence of community can make a critical difference in the lives of those struggling with serious illness, as community mitigates against the debilitating influence of alienation generated by illness. Furthermore, ritual proved to be an under-utilized element in the healing process. Ritual tends to legitimate and make external that which is private and ambiguous. Through ritual people are empowered to name and claim their suffering, and thereby make it real and move out of a place of denial. Ritual also provides opportunities for release and letting go through confession and the sharing of private fears and pains.

The aspect of touch in ritual affirms the wisdom of the ages: that touch is a blessing and contains power, the power of unconditional acceptances, of sympathy, of energy, of support intervening and breaking through the silent wall of alienation. In ritual, the *experience* of illness is legitimated. "You're still a human being, not less so, simply because you are struggling with this problem." I learned how easy it is to gain one's entire identity from illness. I discovered how important it is to move beyond denial into acceptance of diagnosis and disease categories and then to let go of these definitions so they no longer dominate one's definition of self.

The lessons I learned during the years of this experimental ministry confirmed my own experience and taught me about the universal aspects of illness. Many of these themes continue to resound in my work in health and healing.

During the final year of this three-year experiment, I received a call from Judson Memorial Church in Greenwich Village, a church with historic commitments to ministry in the areas of healing and health care. Judson's involvement in health care encompassed women's health and the abortion issue in particular. At the time of my arrival, Judson already housed the Center for Medical Consumers, a free medical library available to any lay person or consumer of medical care who was interested in becoming acquainted with both orthodox and nontraditional literature on diseases, prognosis, and treatment. A joint project of the Center for Medical Consumers and Judson Church that was also under way when I moved to Judson was the Cancer Consultation Service, a free service for emotional support and informational counseling for individuals diagnosed with cancer, and their loved ones. The church also has a committee on healing and health care, which concerns itself with, among other things, new rituals.

In the spring 1983, the AIDS crisis reached epidemic proportions. The press was filled with judgments by religious figures who were convinced that AIDS was God's punishment. In the face of great need, I joined with others from our local community in establishing the AIDS Resource Center, or ARC, designed to provide pastoral and financial services and opportunities for shelter for AIDS patients. I found myself speaking frequently on the theological, political, and pastoral aspects of the illness. A few of us organized and conducted a memorial service in Central Park for those who had died.

During these past years of working in the ministry of healing and health care, based upon my own experience and the experience of others, I have developed some conclusions about the nature of this ministry that I wish to share.

First, I am convinced of the necessity of a theology of *healing*, as opposed to a theology of sickness. Much of our cultural inertia about healing is due to a theological vacuum on this topic. Moreover, so much of what passes for theology on healing simply asserts the relationship between sin and sickness (i.e., sickness is the result of personal sin) and calls for confession. This attitude, needless to say, compounds feelings of judgment for past sins, and does not produce hope. The doctrine of individual retribution shapes most of our unconscious attitudes towards health: "If you're blessed, you have it, and if you're not, you don't." (This is especially true in the AIDS crisis, where individuals are persuaded that their sexual orientation, not their sexual behavior, is to "blame" for their illness.) This sin-sickness assumption must be broken so that the possibility of hope and wholeness can intervene.

Second, the belief that "illness is God's will" is a blueprint for abandonment and a form of cheap grace. If this condition *is* God's will, then why bother? Why struggle to get well? When this line of thinking is challenged, serious questions arise concerning the will of God, the problem of suffering, and the nature of God's power—the doctrine of Omnipotence. Oftentimes, it is much easier to say to a troubled family, "It is God's will," than to examine what God's will might reflect about the nature of this God who presumably wills pain and suffering. Moreover, the absence of a solid theological perspective undermines the healing process, since a coherent philosophy feeds the intellectual, emotional, and spiritual dimensions of a person. It is not simply a "body" that is addressed in the search for healing—or in the presence of illness, for that matter—but the totality of one's being.

It is this totality of being that brings me to my third point. The mind-body duality is real, harmful, and so deeply embedded in our unconscious that we are hardly aware of it. Religion has timidly let medicine assume that illness is purely a material concern and we have abandoned our belief in the "intangibles" in the healing process. In our culture, we see a doctor for a physical sickness, a psychiatrist for a mental ailment, and a clergyperson for a spiritual problem—thereby carving up the integrity of our being. The wisdom of the oldest biblical traditions celebrated the totality of the human being, without indulging in the split between body, mind, and spirit. It seems to me that we indulge in a particular form of cultural sin when we promote a fierce kind of "body-alienation," a fundamental denial and rejection of our original blessing, the gift of our incarnate selves. If we were to take seriously the gift of our incarnate selves, then we would assume responsibility for well-being. The more responsibility we are willing to take, the less we will rely on the authorities in the medical profession to control our well-being.

Fourth, our biblical heritage has much to offer us in our search for health and wholeness. The Hebrew word *Shalom* bespeaks the interconnections of all aspects of life—of peace, well-being, wholeness—health that is collective as well as individual. The interrelationships of all aspects of our lives promoting health and disease cannot be ignored. Health cannot be isolated from environment, nutrition, unemployment. *Shalom*, or health, is not an isolated individual phenomenon.

This emphasis upon wholeness has salvific dimensions, as well, in a culture obsessed with the fantasy of perfection. Wholeness comes as a healing balm to those struggling to accept (rather than *resign*) themselves to a "handicapping" condition. This language I find theologically problematic, since into this imperfect and incomplete creation all of us are born—all of us with wounds, but some whose wounds are more visible than others.

Wholeness is associated with healing in the narratives of Jesus, and so is the concept of salvation. According to Morton Kelsey, it was in the dark ages when the Church eliminated the body from the purview of salvation.[4] Salvation was not intended to be an other-worldly affair, but embodied in the present time. If we were really to take the doctrines of the Incarnation seriously, it would be impossible to deny the body; at the heart of our resistance to healing is a fundamental ambivalence about the body.

The biblical literature and our traditions wrestle with the vexing reality of suffering. Medical treatment of any kind, on any level, that does not take suffering seriously cannot speak to the total healing process. On the other hand, a theology that dismisses suffering with the comment "It is God's will" shallowly refuses to address the places where people live.

Fifth, I have learned that healing is more likely to take shape as a process than an event. It requires commitment and investment, and even a bit of tunnel vision to surrender to its movements, and to learn the lessons illness has to teach. It is rarely a disembodied reality whereby we can get well while hiding the fact of illness, burying it either in shame or neglect or wishful thinking. If possible, one must be in service to the process itself.

Sixth, healing, like suffering, is a mystery. We must never lose sight of that fact, and the Church must intervene in systems and utter this corrective reminder. Without the awareness that healing is a mystery, we can easily indulge in a game of mindless victim blaming in which judgments and recriminations are hurled at the sufferer: "If only he'd do thus and such, then he'd get well." On the other hand, the hubris of medicine must be checked before the idolatry is rampant, idolatry committed in the belief that ultimate control is possible—through technology, or any other avenue, scientific or otherwise. And even in our necrophobic society, death might be the final healing. In the last analysis, God is the author of creation, the architect of mystery, and the source of healing.

Finally, the Church and ministry in these areas are critical in our search for health, healing, and wholeness. Ideally, we have a philosophical and theological approach free from self-aggrandizing interests. The opportunities for education in a parish are endless. It is a prophetic task to intervene into systems of oppression and injustice where one's health depends on one's wealth. Nonprofessional, low-cost, and empowering health practices can be taught and shared in faith communities. People can be educated to take responsibility for their health, to trust their bodies, and to learn about the invisible and ambiguous aspects of health. In the pastoral ministry, we can enable one another to become historians of one another's illness, breaking through the isolation. We can resurrect the sacrament of touch, revere our embodied selves, and rejoice in wholeness—not perfection—as our call to life. We can empower one another to be responsible as consumers and as care givers. Our healing is not an abstraction, it begins with our beings. And in our healing and our self-care, we might begin to discover some secrets to the *shalom* for our world.

Notes

1. Morton Kelsey, *Christianity & Healing (New York: Harper & Row, 1973).*

2. Eugenia Lee Hancock, Introduction to "Proposal for Ministry in Healing and Health Care," submitted to the Health Ministries of the Program Agency, United Presbyterian Church of the U.S.A., New York, 1979.

3. Hancock, Brochure on Healing Services "Introduction to Services," Central Presbyterian Church, 1980, New York.

4. Kelsey, *Christianity & Healing,* p. 203.

MINISTERING TO WOMEN IN PRISON

Margaret Ellen Traxler

"I can't be sorry for the crime. I've tried and I know God won't forgive me if I have no sorrow." Abbie spoke with intensity. She was a "lifer," sentenced to prison for shooting her son-in-law, who had physically abused Abbie's daughter for over a decade.

I put my arm around her and moved over to the corner of the classroom where we had just completed our class. "Can you pray for him?" I asked. "It's impossible to pray for that brute," she replied, her anguish visible. "But I want to know that God forgives me."

"Let's pray together, now," I said, and we sat down and quietly began.

During the weeks of Abbie's healing, I often asked myself

Sister Margaret Ellen Traxler is director of the Institute of Women Today in Chicago. The institute was founded in 1974 "to search for the religious and historical roots of women's liberation." She also has served as the executive director of the National Catholic Conference for Interracial Justice. She is the founder of the National Coalition of American Nuns and the cofounder of the Interreligious Conference on Soviet Jewry. Sister Traxler is a School Sister of Notre Dame and holds a master's degree from Notre Dame University.

whether I would not have been driven to the same action. Yet, in this and similar incidents, I keep asking myself, "How can I help others transmute life's pain and burdens into a spiritual and prayerful direction without the empty promise of pie in the sky?" Achieving this is what ministry is to me.

Jesus cured Peter's mother-in-law, and she immediately rose up and ministered to them. Ministry is service out of love, service based on the Gospel matrix of the life and example of Jesus. As a Catholic woman I am denied ordination; yet I must find ways of ministering without the right of administering sacramental graces or offering official worship.

An incident from my childhood illustrates an example of true ministry. At the time I was about twelve years old, in about the sixth grade. We lived in a small town in southern Minnesota. Some friends and I were playing in the city park that borders along the Minnesota River. It was getting late in the afternoon, and I knew that I would be expected home for supper. A child who had joined us in our afternoon games said to me, "We have no food for our supper." I asked, "How come?" and she said, "Our dad didn't make any sales."

Her family lived in a small mobile home, which they took from town to town as her father gathered willow fronds from the river banks and made garden furniture, lawn tables, and chairs to sell in the town. When business dwindled, they moved on to another city. I was troubled by her words, and when I went home I told my mother about the kids at city park who had no food for supper. She looked at me and asked, "Can you show me where they live?" Before getting into her car, we went to our basement vegetable room and filled some baskets with food and then drove down to the park.

What I remember most is not so much the joy of the children when they saw the food, but the love and solicitude my mother showed for the other mother. Though strangers, they embraced. We set the food baskets down, and my mother promised to return after our two families had eaten our evening meal. My mother drove down again later and visited for several hours. As we children played in the park during the hours of dusk, I looked into the small trailer home and saw my mother tenderly holding hands across the table with the weeping woman.

The next morning my father called a nearby town to ask friends there about possible business for rattan furniture and a city park for the mobile home. These visitors felt my parents' love for them. I learned ministry was more than feeding the hungry; it expressed true love of neighbor, which these neighbors felt.

Our challenge is to love people we serve and to have them feel this love. If they do not feel our love, I believe that our love is flawed. People felt the love Jesus held for them. Jesus loved beyond the concern that he had as he sent his workers out "to preach the kingdom . . . to go to the lost . . . to bring the message . . . cure the sick, raise the dead, cleanse the lepers and cast out devils" (Matt. 10:5–13). When Jesus reminded, "therefore do not be anxious saying 'what shall we drink' or 'what shall we wear'," he was not telling us to let people starve or go homeless, nor was he asking the poor not to worry. Directly following this text is the directive to seek justice and the added footnote that "sufficient for the day is its own trouble" (Matt. 6:31, 34).

I have served incarcerated women for ten years. The Institute of Women Today, which I founded to work with women in prisons and jails, has many volunteers and teachers from our interfaith sponsoring groups. Our first rule is that we must come as servants and as those who bring love. Jesus described himself as a servant and warned his disciples to "lord it not over those they served." To be clergy, ordained minister under whatever title, does not grant honorific status which then forever sets the person apart.[1]

The servant who leads must bring three levels of love and service to her ministry. First is a true love for self, without which there can be no healthy love for those who are served. Second, in loving and serving those to whom we minister, we bring that wholeness and maturity that is borne out of a recognition of our own dignity and self-worth. Third, this love and appreciation of self and of our neighbor forms a spiritual and actual community of love, which serves as a Christian design for true Gospel ministry. If self-concept is flawed, this lack of wholeness prevents spiritual growth and impedes mature exercise of sacred ministry.

A woman in prison asked me, "Do you think that God will forgive me?" When I assured her that our God was one of love and mercy she replied, "But no one has ever loved me, so why shouldn't I doubt?" She had no human experience of love on which to base the concept of Isaiah, "You are precious in my eyes" (Isa. 43:4). Love of self and true appreciation of one's dignity are so often confused with self-conceit.

With this healthy self-image we can understand that we have something to give others, and this helps us extend our love and care to one another. By this shall all know that we are disciples. Community is based on mutual love and trust. If there is true community spirit, the witness of it sings without attention being drawn to it.

Search for community is the thirst of all normal persons; and it is in a faith body that one would hope to find identity and belonging. In the world of corrections, it is the surest hope for conversion and decisions for new beginnings. Forming community with his followers was also the desire of Jesus. His invitation "to come aside and rest awhile" provided his disciples time to get to know one another, as did the retreats on the mountains and in the desert.

There are many circles of women in prison who have formed true community of sharing and mutuality. If there is a cottage system of living in the prison, community grows more easily within that circle. One group I know prays together at six o'clock each morning. Because they love to sing, they go to the basement recreation room. They meet again for evening prayer, for sharing, and for meditation.

"This is the first time I've felt part of a group, needed by them and supported," said June. Like the majority of women in prison, she had known little parental love, no affirmation from family or friends. Through the first experience of community, June had been introduced to prayer. Community experience was her first introduction to serious search for prayer and union. In sharing sisterhood with a small group of women prisoners, June discovered dignity and acceptance for the first time.

While all people are in the pilgrim search for meaning, none thirst so deeply as some of the women in prison I have known. Prisoners are truly the *anawim*. Defined in Scripture as the most abject, the unwanted and despised, the *anawim* are the preferred people of God. When I told the women in Cook County Jail how God held them in preference as *anawim*, one woman responded, "We should tell that to the circuit judge!" Whether or not the judges would care, however, God's love for the *anawim* must be remembered by those who minister to prisoners in loving service.

The prisoners' concept of God as judge is largely based on their courtroom experience of judges. It is little wonder, then, that many prison women conceive of God only as a judge who demands reparation. It is hard to pray with this burden. The concept of God as a tender and loving friend is hardest of all to convey. The police, the courts, and the corrections systems to the prisoner represent a merciless, legalistic, unyielding, almighty arm of the law. In conceptualizing God, the prisoner who has been in the grip of that law cannot picture God as the spirit of love and mercy, but only as a forboding dignitary related to our legal systems. Our ministry must personify for all the New Commandment given by Jesus that everyone "will know that you are my disciples, if you have love for one another" (John 13:35).

The Institute of Women Today sponsors many levels of service programs for women in many jails and prisons. These offerings range from building skills such as carpentry and plumbing, to classes in parenting, Progoff intensive journal writing, and street law. We also operate Sisterhouse on Chicago's Westside for women coming out of any prison, offering them a place to stay until they feel really ready to return to mainstream society. Whatever we offer, we always try to include classes in Scripture, because it is so often through the freeing word of revelation that such women can find themselves.

I teach one of these classes, and I consider it my reward for coordinating all the other activities, volunteers, and teachers. Using Janice Nunnally Cox's book, *Foremothers, Women in the Bible*,[2] we study all of the women in the Bible and try to find the virtues of every woman depicted there. It isn't hard for prison women to see how such historic figures as Jezebel or the daughters of Lot were caught in their webs of conspiracy.

"Lot's daughters couldn't be anybody without sons," said Audrey. "How could they have sons up in hiding away in the mountains alone with their father?" replied Vicky. "So who is to blame them for seducing the old man?" asked Audrey. "And before doing that they had to give him too much to drink," reminded Vicky. "It was a man's world where men called all the shots and the family deserves credit for running from Sodom and Gomorrah," concluded Audrey. And so on with the great litany of heroines such as Dinah, Tamar, Jochebed, and Rahab.

I have learned much of love and understanding from women in prison. Their earthiness and reverence combine to create a spirit of holy dialogue in classes. One night as we opened with prayer and meditation, Rene said, "We can't begin class." Surprised, I said, "Why not?" Rene looked pointedly at Jackie. Jackie looked down at her hands folded over her open Bible. Finally, she said, "I've had a fight with Sally." Rene enjoined, "We need reconciliation." A silence ensued. Jackie slowly turned and asked forgiveness. Sally stood up, and the two embraced. Then everyone stood up and began embracing all around, and I even found myself in it all. But that was not the end. After we finally settled down and I thought that the class could begin, Rene asked, "Couldn't we sing a song of thanksgiving?"

These women bring me to my knees each time I encounter their world of bars and recriminations. We spend weekends with them in prison in teams of five to six women professionals ranging from psychologists to lawyers. One Sunday, after we had spent three days in a state prison with about two hundred women, some of the residents walked us to the last barred door. They stopped and one of them, Mary Jane, said, "We took a little collection for you all." She handed us an envelope, adding, "It takes money for you to come all this way." Later we counted their alms of $37.40, a small sum that meant as much as the generous gifts that keep our Institute of Women Today on the roads for prisons everywhere.

Another such example was given by women in a southern prison, where we sponsor a modest prison industry with profits going to the women's private prison account. In fulfilling a contract for denim shoulder bags, we provided all the materials including the sewing machines. For each bag, the maker received three dollars. Minni had a four-year-old son who needed leg braces. The women in Minnie's cellblock made one hundred bags, pooled the profits, and handed them in under Minnie's name. Some weeks later little Ronnie visited his mother in prison, and each woman welcomed him as her own because the braces that the little one wore represented the money each woman had earned, the "fruit of her own hands."

We have teams of eight to ten women volunteers with us on our weekends in prison. Those skilled in crafts hold several classes in quilting and other sewing folk arts. The quilting has already led to a thriving industry in Mississippi's Parchman Prison. Other courses that interest residents are arts, ceramics, macrame, and citizen's law. The lawyers who teach the law classes also interview women who need help in writing grievance reports, appeals, briefs, and other legal writing. Sometimes our attorneys even have to explain to the women just how they broke the law and why the jury made the decision that it made.

When it comes to official worship, women prisoners unfortunately suffer the same patriarchal system as their sisters at large. Indeed, the worship experience of women in prison is as male-dominated as their bitter stories of courts and corrections. I know of no adequate or satisfactory opportunities for women in prison to enter into vital, living social worship. Those of our own Catholic faith rarely have official representatives in women's prisons. In one southern state prison of eight thousand men and women, a priest visits bimonthly— and then for men only. When Catholic women ask me when their turn will come, I try to help by forming committees to organize their own prayer services with choir and Scripture readings.

In one large women's jail, we organized such a prayer service with the residents. Previously, when there had been an occasional mass, about ten women attended. Our Scripture service—with a homily, readings, silent meditation, and the residents' own choir—drew about one hundred women. Hearing of the success of our "packed house," the priest decided to come more regularly. Ironically, because he was the official chaplain, our own liturgies had to be discontinued, and the congregation gradually dwindled back to the handful of former times. The need for women ministers and priests is all too evident!

An ongoing test of faith for prison ministry, as with all ministry, is the danger of internalizing the sufferings of others. The Institute of Women Today has several full-time women advocates who do for the residents what they cannot do for themselves or their families, and these advocates daily try to remain objective when hearing and seeing the anguish of others. Psychologists say to us, "be clinical" when listening to the pain of others. Being clinical helps prevent internalizing the suffering of others, but while this may be possible for the clinician, I doubt that a true minister can ever be completely clinical.

In his day, Jesus knew flat or unleavened bread; but he also knew the power of leaven. The difference between sterile services and vital ministering, between doing a job and fulfilling the call to active ministry, is found in the one word: love. Jesus believed this word, love, to be like the leaven "which a woman took and hid in three measures of flour, til it was all leavened" (Matt. 13:33). I see it as the tender love we bring to others in the name of Jesus. With this love, the promise is that "you shall receive power when the Holy Spirit has come upon you; and you shall be my witness" (Acts 1:8). The poor know a true witness, they also know the false ones. They readily discern the trappings of other kinds of power: real estate, long impressive cars, and position "at the gates of the city." It is the leaven of love that communicates the Gospel and gives life and meaning to the message and life of Jesus. Through a life of prayer, the minister with or without ordination comes to perceive and then live the intense ministry based in the example of the life and testament of Jesus.

Notes

1. The humbling revelations of the growth of clergy power are given by Pulitzer prize-winning historian Barbara Tuchman in *The Distant Mirror* (New York: Alfred A. Knopf, 1978), and of the excesses of such power in her latest work, *March to Folly* (New York: Alfred A. Knopf, 1984)

2. Janice Nunnally Cox, *Foremothers, Women in the Bible* (New York: Seabury Press, 1981).

COLLEAGUES
IN MARRIAGE
AND MINISTRY

Linda McKiernan–Allen and Ronald J. Allen

Coming out of the penetrating February wind, we found ourselves engulfed in the soggy warmth of the hotel's finest artificial tropics. The sixty men and women milling around the chlorinated waterfall were clergy and spouses from the Nebraska Region of the Christian Church (Disciples of Christ). It was the midwinter retreat, the first since our arrival in the area six months earlier.

Friends greeted one another, and name tags were handed out. As we pinned on the colored paper squares, one of the men asked, "Aren't you that new couple up to Grand Island?" Our affirmative response led immediately to the

The Rev. Linda McKiernan-Allen and the Rev. Ronald J. Allen are co-ministers of First Christian Church in Grand Island, Nebraska. They are both graduates of Phillips University in Enid, Oklahoma. Ms. McKiernan-Allen took her seminary training at Princeton Theological Seminary, Mr. Allen at Union Theological Seminary, New York. He also holds a Ph.D. in New Testament from Drew University.

question, "How's it working with both of you in the church?" Asked in tones ranging from curious to skeptical, the inquiry was repeated a dozen times in the next twenty-four hours. It is that way at most gatherings where we appear for the first time.

Clergy and laity both want to see "behind the door." Our ministry is one instance of the phenomenon of clergy couples in the church, and in this chapter we try to indicate something of the connections between our marriage and ministry.

A clergy couple is a woman and a man, married to one another, both theologically trained, ordained, and engaged in ministry. Put more simply, it is two ministers who are married to each other.

The Salvation Army has been ordaining husband and wife teams in the United States since 1880.[1] Pentecostal churches have been ordaining women, some of whom have been part of clergy couples, since the early twentieth century.[2] However, significant numbers of clergy couples have entered mainline Protestant denominations only since the early 1970s when women began enrolling in seminaries in significant numbers. As the decade drew to a close, there were some 850 clergy couples in this group of denominations. United Methodists had the largest number, with 300 couples, but the United Church of Christ and the Christian Church (Disciples of Christ) led in the number of clergy couples as a percentage of the total clergy.[3]

Clergy couples, then, make up less than 1 percent of all ordained clergy in the United States, though if current trends continue, their numbers are expected to double by the mid-1980s.[4] As might be expected of a new development, the majority of clergy couples tend to be young. In a study done in the late 1970s, 85 percent of the women and 79 percent of the men were age thirty-nine or younger.[5]

Clergy couples vary in the types of ministries performed, both by the individuals and among the couples themselves. The type of ministry on which we are focusing is that in which both partners serve one congregation, each partner on a part-time basis. Often each works half-time, thus making one full-time position. We are employed three-quarters time each.

This arrangement allows time for partners to pursue interests beyond the local ministry as well as to share home responsibilities. Child rearing, caring for aged parents, and household chores can be handled in an egalitarian manner instead of according to traditional male and female roles. In opting for this lifestyle, many clergy couples are involved in an experiment which holds real potential for a shift in our thinking about the nuclear family as well as the shape of the church's ministry.[6]

Most clergy couples who serve together are in an equal relationship as co-pastors. In a few instances one is designated senior minister with the other as his or her associate. It is, of course, difficult for some members of a local church to grasp the concept of two ministers who have equal responsibility, and they may persist in turning to the man as "the" minister. Ironically, in our parish the members who had the most difficulty accepting the notion of co-ministry were the younger people. The older members, who had grown up in a rural environment and observed their parents working together on the farm, were more easily able to transfer that sense of teamwork to the co-pastorate.

Parishes of two or more churches can be served by clergy couples. Sometimes these couples are co-pastors, but in other situations each member of the team is responsible for certain churches. In other cases each is in pastoral ministry, but the two are in separate congregations. This is a popular option when the individuals belong to separate denominations; it also works well when the two find it difficult to work together in the same congregation.

A large number of clergy couples have separate ministries altogether. One might be a chaplain and the other a local pastor. In a few cases among clergy couples with a specialized focus, the two people share one position. For instance, one denominational position or one teaching appointment may be divided between them.

Clergy couples thus model dual career options for all families. Such a model can be important to families that are in the midst of changing traditional role patterns. When a parsonage family is successfully managing such an arrangement, other families can see how it works on a day-to-day basis. In addition to being a model, the pastors can be trusted counselors on this issue. And, happily, the opposite situation also holds true: Families that have been managing two careers successfully, in many cases for years, can be instructive to the clergy couple.

Our own pilgrimage began in April 1977, when the First Christian Church (Disciples of Christ) in Grand Island, Nebraska, called us. The story leading to the call actually began in the fall of 1976, as we worked together on our dossier. That writing project gave us an opportunity for gut-level dialogue with one another about our ministry, forcing us to clarify what we thought, felt, hoped, and dreamed for our ministry.

Despite the difficulty of two people trying to compose one autobiographical piece, we accomplished the job. The one thing we agreed on, and which our dossier indicated unmistakably, was that we sought a position together. In addition to the basic information, we included an addendum (titled "Our Shared Vision") which described how we saw the nuts-and-bolts operation of our ministry. We explained carefully that we wanted to work together, each being paid a separate salary. Our specific talents were described, as well as how we saw those talents complementing one another to form a more complete ministry than most individual ministers could provide.

We knew that in order to sell the idea of a two-minister family, we had to be clear about the potential advantage for the local congregation. Further, throughout the dossier and the addendum we avoided the use of unfamiliar jargon (such as clergy couple, co-pastorate, or team ministry). Instead, we wrote out what we meant, thereby clarifying the ideas for ourselves and for anyone who might read the material.

We were fortunate to have personal relationships with our denominational officials who facilitate ministerial placement. We discovered that while our national staff was very supportive of clergy couple ministry, many middle judicatory officials (regional ministers) were still a little foggy about the concept. In our denomination it is the regional ministers who put dossiers into the hands of local pulpit committees, so we wanted the dossier to be a tool for their education as well as an introduction of us.

When our interview at Grand Island was confirmed, we tried to imagine ourselves in the place of the pulpit committee. What would they want to know? We rightly anticipated that they would want to see how labor would be divided. Handmade charts showing how we thought we would divide ministerial responsibilities gave the committee something concrete with which to work. We drew freely from our reservoir of stories illustrating how successfully co-ministry was working elsewhere.

An important pastoral concern of the committee was whether our marriage could withstand the mix with ministry. We were glad to report that while few data are available, the divorce rate and the number of serious marital problems do not appear to be higher among clergy couples than among the ordinary clergy population. We explained that because of the small number of clergy couples and the newness of the concept, we often are watched with unusual curiosity. So when a problem develops, it may appear to the outsider to be more important than it really is.

After we met with the pulpit committee, led Sunday morning worship, and participated in a variety of meetings to get acquainted with the congregation, the church voted 228 to 1 to call us. The one dissenter was concerned not about our role as a clergy couple, but about our youth. (We were both under thirty.) In the congregational system of polity the regional and general church offices are strictly advisory and have no authority over placement; the congregation alone makes the final decision. The problems of placement are different in an appointive system, such as the United Methodist Church. There the responsibility of matching pastor and church belongs to the bishop and district superintendent. Such officials often are concerned with the church's potential difficulty in meeting its obligation of a guaranteed appointment when couples may want to serve in the same church or the same geographical area.

Our agreement with the Grand Island church is based on one-and-a-half time employment divided equally between us. We determine the elusive three-fourths as follows: Each working day is divided into five modules of two hours each. Each morning is two modules, each afternoon two, and each evening is normally one module. A check with area clergy indicated that full-time employment is about forty-eight hours (or twenty-four modules) a week. Three-quarters time would then be eighteen modules. In practice our enthusiasm, occasional lack of organization, and unwillingness to say no often result in longer work weeks.

It is often difficult to separate "work time" from "time off." Often we find ourselves talking over church business when working in the garden. Dinner can become the occasion for replaying memorable encounters. Social events with friends from the church often find us talking church business.

But with this agreement we believe the ministry of First Christian Church may have more strengths than it would have with a single minister. Two people are likely to have more strengths than a lone pastor and thus compensate for deficiencies. In the same vein, congregations which normally would have only one minister can have access to twice the program resources. But we have to be careful, for with two energy cells it is easy to overprogram and leave both ourselves and the church weary.

Two equal salaries, two health-care premiums (which are less expensive than a family policy), and equal pension fund deposits are included in our agreement. We have separate offices in the church building and share one (often flustered) part-time secretary. The following table compares expenditures for single minister and multiple staff situations with expenditures for clergy couples. The major saving, of course, is in housing.

The congregation has allowed us carte blanche as we have developed the shape of our ministry. The previous ministry was carried on by one full-time minister, so the congregation did not have any experience with a two-person staff.

COST COMPARISONS (1979)

	1 Minister	Clergy Couple (½-time each)	2 Ministers (full-time)	Clergy Couple (¾-time each)	Clergy Couple (full-time each)
Salary	$12,000	$12,000	$24,000	$18,000	$24,000
Housing	4,000	4,000	8,000	4,000	4,000
Pension*	2,100	2,100	4,200	3,150	4,200
Car	2,000	2,000	4,000	3,000	4,000
Convention	500	500	1,000	750	1,000
Health care	1,000	1,000	2,000	1,000	1,000
Education	700	700	1,400	1,000	1,400
TOTAL	$22,300	$22,300	$44,600	$30,900	$39,600

*Pension deposit is calculated on 13 percent of salary and housing.

✓ Flexibility is a key to managing our relationship. We have respect for each other and for what we each can and cannot do. While there are always surprises and changes, we have something of an initial advantage over the normal ministerial team. When the moving van pulls into the parking lot, the clergy couple already is operating at a high trust level, with built-in knowledge of each other's strengths and weaknesses.

We do not divide every task in half. Because of our individual needs for a sense of accomplishment and the church's need for continuity of leadership, one person follows a project from beginning to end. Once Ron begins to prepare a sermon, Linda does not, without an invitation, try to change the thrust of it. Once Linda has started a community project, Ron does not make uninvited suggestions about how to do it. Rarely do we attend the same committee meetings.

Separate responsibilities also mean that we do not spend all of our working time together. We have regular hours in separate offices, and often we are calling at the same time but in different parts of town. Only occasionally do we treat ourselves to making a call together. Neither do we take all our time off together, for we each pursue our own interests.

In an unfortunate incident during our first week in Grand

Island, we discovered that we individually had accepted dinner invitations from two different families on the same night. On another notorious occasion Linda was talking on the phone when Ron unceremoniously ripped the phone from her hands and in an energized voice began to "correct" the information Linda was passing along. We have since learned not to speak for one another or embarrass each other.

We also have learned not only to live with but to celebrate our differences, both in theology and in our understanding of ministry. Ron appreciates revivalistic and charismatic expressions of piety more than Linda, who is by nature more quiet and formal. This occasionally causes tension in the relationship when Ron wants to sing gospel songs at the same time Linda would put on the albs and bring in a crucifer. Fortunately, both of our theologies, rooted in biblical experience and nourished by the notion of the greatness and grandeur of God, can embrace such far-flung differences.

In fact, we now believe the congregation is enriched by such a varying diet. Our congregation has three different kinds of worship service offered at different times each Sunday: A traditional midwestern Protestant service (which one of our elders characterizes as "dignified informality"); a charismatic experience with the music projected on a screen and accompanied by handclapping, spontaneous expressions of praise, and occasional verbal punctuation; and a loose, spontaneous service with Avery and Marsh kinds of music, communion in the round, and pastor-congregation dialogue during the sermon.

This pluralism does have its drawbacks. Intentionally or unintentionally, some members try to get us to divide against ourselves. Pluralism leads to power blocks, and sometimes we are the fulcrums on which these blocks work their leverage. Still, in the language of Paul, we are "fellow workers in Christ" (Rom. 16:3). We are visible and vocal each week in worship. Normally, one preaches and reads Scripture while the other offers the pastoral prayer, introduces communion, tells a children's story, and works with the lay worship leader.

Variation in styles of preaching and worship leadership are refreshing for the congregation. Furthermore, with a regular break in preaching, we have time for reading and reflection, which are important for fresh preaching. The week-by-week presence of a colleague as a critic helps. Ron has a Ph.D. with an interdisciplinary focus in preaching. While both of us think of him as the stronger and more consistent preacher and interpreter of Scripture, the congregation does not share the discrimination. Indeed, they respond to us as equals in the pulpit. Linda brings a stronger social conscience and the courage and sensitivity necessary to express it. Our preaching is thus better balanced than if only one of us were in the pulpit.

Generally, the congregation's response to our co-ministry has been positive, with both men and women expressing appreciation for the coordination of the services and teamwork. We each baptize and welcome new members. We are team workers in program as well. We have separate committee responsibilities, which are assigned according to ability and interest as follows:

DIVISION OF LABOR

Ron	Joint Responsibility	Linda
Evangelism	Worship	Community action
Membership	Education	World outreach
Property	Pastor-parish relations	Stewardship

We each do about half of the pastoral calling on members and shut-ins; Linda does most of the hospital visitation, and Ron concentrates on evangelism. Funeral services and weddings are handled by whoever answers the phone unless the family has a particular request. In emergency situations we are twice as available as a single minister because we *can* be in two places at once.

Counseling appointments are accepted by both, usually at the request of the counselee. Often we work together in premarital and marriage counseling. Counseling alternatives are broadened as members of the congregation and community are given choices according to personality and sex. Both women and men appreciate the possibility of working with a "same gender" counselor at one point and "cross gender" or "joint gender" at another.

For special events we agree on responsibility on the basis of interest, time available, and ability. Sometimes we have to fight for the "plum" jobs. We have been trained jointly to lead marriage communication labs. Ron oversees an annual week of renewal, while Linda is involved with the CROP walk and Church World Service.

By working three-quarters time, we are able to devote significant amounts of time and energy to personal projects. Ron writes, tries to keep afloat in the shifting tides of New Testament research and preaching, and is available for free-lance Bible study leadership. Linda works with the regional and general levels of the church and enjoys creative aspects of homemaking. These activities enrich the life of the congregation without robbing it of pastoral leadership.

An important fixed event in our week is the Monday morning staff meeting. Because we count on at least an hour of time together, focused on our work, many small irritations and concerns can then be aired without interrupting the flow of the week. Of course, some bombshells must be dealt with when they explode, but many others can be stored and vented later. That staff meeting helps curb the 11 P.M. bedside staff meetings. It also clarifies responsibilities and direction for the week. Inevitably we come away encouraged and renewed; we feel that we are working together for the common good.

There are, of course, problem areas. It can be difficult for each of us to maintain his or her identity. Some members see not Ron and Linda but "the kids." Calls are frequently concluded with the parishioner saying, "Next time, please bring your husband (or wife)." Mistakes and successes are occasionally attributed not to the individual who is responsible but to the team.

Believe it or not, we can have too much togetherness. Sometimes it seems as though we are together everywhere but in the bathroom.

Occasionally, competition gets in the way of ministry. Each morning we swim or run at the YMCA and record our mileage. We race to see who can reach the Five Hundred Mile Club first and have even been known to double-check the other's addition. When this friendly sense of competition is transferred to a church program or sermon, we sometimes find ourselves pushing our individual interests as if God has a giant chart in the sky on which points are recorded. Awareness of this tendency enables us to relieve each other by chiding or confrontation.

Another problem comes when the church does not know how to express dissatisfaction with one partner's performance. Sometimes the fear of damaging the clergy couple's marriage inhibits parishioners from making an appropriate criticism of one partner's ministry. On the other side, each of us must sometimes tolerate what seems to be the inferior ministry of the other. How do you look interested when your partner preaches a sermon that needs another day or two in the study? At the same time, we are sometimes unable to separate criticism of one from criticism of the other. Unnecessary pain results.

Such occasions can present an opportunity to model conflict management for the congregation. We do not try unnecessarily to hide our disagreements and disappointments from the congregation, though we do not wear them like ribbons either. We try to share our differences with one another and with boards and committees in situations which allow for free expression and growth, avoiding win-lose situations. We demonstrate in our own lives that a difference of opinion does not mean that someone must put his or her Bible on the shelf and go home.

Because of our common commitment to marriage and ministry, we enjoy wholeness of life. Our lives are cut from one piece of colorful fabric. Though there can be confusion between home and work, mutual understanding of the sources of tension and pain leads to strength in resolving them. We are open with each other in a way which is sometimes difficult for conventional colleagues, especially those in hierarchial situations, to understand. At the same time, there are confidences that must be respected and not shared even with our partner.

We are free to work with each other when inspired. Few others would feel free to call a colleague when an idea sparks at 2 A.M. While Linda has serious questions about the contribution Ron makes at that hour, she can feed her own enthusiasm by rolling him around in bed with, "Look at this!" He, on the other hand, can have a new thought at 6 A.M. and find someone who will at least say, "Go to it."

Most of our conversations about our ministry, with both laity and clergy, center on the practical side. An older member of the congregation was the first to put us on the firing line. "I don't remember reading about any of these 'clergy couples' in the Bible. Are you sure it's all right?" Asked in more and less sophisticated ways by a variety of questioners, the query often is a cover for underlying insecurity about the place of women in ministry and about the relationship of husbands and wives. Our experience has been that such hesitation usually is caused by a lack of exposure. But some people have a deep-seated theological anxiety which needs to be taken seriously.

We frankly admitted to the woman who confronted us that the Old Testament contains few, if any, examples of husbands and wives sharing leadership of the people of God. There were no women priests, although there are instances of charismatically inspired women rising to the pinacle of leadership.

In turning to the New Testament, we pointed out that while there were no husband-wife teams among the twelve apostles, there were women who, breaking with commonly accepted Jewish practice of the time, not only followed Jesus but supported him and the twelve financially (Luke 8:1-3, 10:38-42, 23:49; Mark 13:10).

We stressed that both men and women were leaders in the early church and that there are several instances of men and women sharing leadership. Among the first of such couples were Priscilla and Aquila (Rom. 16:3-5; 1 Cor. 16:19). Luke depicts the couple as missionaries with Paul (Acts 18:1-3) who jointly instructed Apollos (Acts 18:26).

In Paul's time, most churches met in homes, and it is likely that many were headed by husbands and wives working together. Paul mentions the following by name: Andronicus and Junias (if "Junias" is feminine, Rom. 16:7), Philologus and Julia (Rom. 16:15), Philemon and Apphia (Philem. 1:2). Though admittedly there is scant information about how the spouses shared labor and leadership, it is noteworthy that women and men, working together, are acknowledged as leaders of the household of faith.

Those who object to the ministry of clergy couples on biblical grounds usually cite the household codes of Ephesians 5:21–32; Colossians 3:18–4:1; 1 Peter 3:1–7; the instructions to the overenthusiastic woman in 1 Corinthians 14:33b–36; or the insistence that women are not mentioned among the leadership of the churches in 1 Timothy 3:1–13 or Titus 1:5–16. These and related questions have been dealt with by responsible interpreters on Scripture on behalf of the women's movement. In dealing with lay people and suspicious pastors, we have found it inadequate to bring out Galatians 3:28 (". . . there is neither male nor female . . ."), followed by statements like "Things were different then." It is confusing to suggest that 1 Corinthians 14:33b–36 may not have been written by Paul. In any case, that approach does not touch the problem of the text's meaning for today, since those verses are in the canon whether or not they were written by Paul.

We have found that genuine dialogue can be opened as we discuss the historical context of the churches to which the passages were written. It is natural to point out that women were in positions of leadership in the early church and are remembered as the first witnesses of the Resurrection.

When women are in visible positions of leadership in our society, it says to the world: "In this church women are first class." Having both women and men share leadership provides an inclusive view of the nature of God. Recent studies have pointed out feminine images of the divine. These hitherto neglected themes are an important corrective to the dominant (and often damaging) picture of God as patriarch.

Here, as elsewhere, clergy couples may provide the occasion for fresh, more adequate ways of thinking and working in the church.

While our ministry in Grand Island provides both the church and us with rich opportunities, there may come a time when our work is no longer effective or when another call offers challenges that seem appropriate to our continuing growth. But it may be more complicated for us to leave than it was to come. One of us may be ready to move (possibly into another form of ministry) while the other wishes to remain. The church may want one of us to leave but the other to continue. We both might sense that our productivity has ended but be unable to locate another position in which we can share marriage and ministry.

While there are questions prior to coming, during a ministry, and facing a move, the most important thing for us is the joy of continuing to work with the one we love. In ordained ministry and marriage two signs of God's grace stand side by side in Christian community.

Notes

1. Robert Sandall, *The History of the Salvation Army* (London: Thomas Nelson, 1950), vol. 2, pp. 161, 228.

2. John Thomas Nichol, *Pentecostalism* (New York: Harper & Row, 1976), pp. 59–63, 120. Cf. Richard Quebedeaux, *The New Charismatics* (Garden City, N.Y.: Doubleday, 1976), p. 32.

3. Nancy Jo von Lackum and John von Lackum, III, *Clergy Couples: A Report on Clergy Couples and the Ecumenical Clergy Couples Consultation* (New York: National Council of Churches, 1979), p. 4.

4. Ibid.

5. Ibid., p. 5.

6. Ibid. See pp. 14–18 for a summary of a presentation by Peggy and Bill Way at an ecumenical clergy couples consultation in which they suggest that clergy couples model possible alternatives to the problems of authority, community, and identity in church and society.